MAKING DISCIPLES

MAKING DISCIPLES

A Handbook of Christian Moral Formation

Timothy E. O'Connell

A Crossroad Herder Book
The Crossroad Publishing Company
New York

The Crossroad Publishing Company
370 Lexington Avenue, New York, NY 10017

Printed in the United States of America

Library of Congress Cataloging-in-Publication Data

O'Connell, Timothy E.
   Making disciples : a handbook of Christian moral formation / Timothy E. O'Connell.
      p.   cm.
   "Crossroad Herder book."
   Includes bibliographical references.
   ISBN 0-8245-1727-X (pbk.)
   1. Christian education—Philosophy. 2. Christian ethics—Catholic authors. 3. Catholic Church—Education. 4. Moral development. 5. Discipling (Christianity). 6. Spiritual formation.   I. Title.
BV1464.026 1998
268'.82—dc21   97-37558
                                                 CIP

1 2 3 4 5 6 7 8 9 10 02 01 00 99 98

L.L.

Contents

Part 3
The Other Venue of Experience

Part 4
Strategies for Pastoral Ministry

Acknowledgments

AS I EXPLAIN IN THE INTRODUCTION, THIS BOOK HAS BEEN percolating for over a decade. The length of my attention to this topic has only multiplied the gifts I have received and the gratitude I must articulate.

I begin by acknowledging a research leave provided by Loyola University Chicago in 1994, which allowed me to move from general insight to scholarly detail. This generous support proved to be critical in advancing this project. I remain profoundly grateful.

In recent years, I have been blessed with several opportunities to teach courses incorporating my emerging understanding of the matters of this book. My students in the Institute of Pastoral Studies at Loyola have confirmed the accuracy of Oscar Hammerstein's "by your students you'll be taught." Among many who deserve my thanks, I must identify Ms. Barbara Outly, an experienced religious educator who is the source for several of the ideas in chapter 12. I have also been very lucky to have had the help of two graduate assistants whose skillful editorial assistance was matched by their insightful suggestions. To Meaghan Hoddinott-Pottorff and Melinda Lupfer, my thanks. And my colleagues on the faculty of the Institute of Pastoral Studies have provided me the gift of one formal discussion of many of the book's key ideas and many informal—but extremely helpful—personal conversations.

I also gratefully acknowledge the gracious permission of several publishers to reprint charts on which they hold copyright: to Paulist Press for the chart on p. 47; to the American Psychological Association for the chart on p. 49, itself a modified version of a chart published by Alfred A. Knopf and Co.; to Alfred A. Knopf and Co., for extending to me the permission they originally gave to the APA for that modification; to W. H. Sadlier Publishing Co., for the chart on p. 51; and to W. W. Norton, for the chart on p. 48. I also wish to note that all scriptural quotations are taken from the New Revised Standard Version.

It is very difficult to sort out the sources of one's insights. This is especially so when one has been pursuing a question for as long as I have and has explored it from so many angles. Some notable sources must nonetheless be named, in fairness and with sincere gratitude. The overarching model for this work, locating one's values in experience, with a special role for imagination and community, can be traced to two wonderful books, both of which influenced me greatly: Daniel Maguire's *The Moral Choice* (Garden City, N.Y.: Doubleday, 1978) and Andrew Greeley and Mary Greeley Durkin's *How to Save the Catholic Church* (New York: Viking Penguin, 1984). I cannot exaggerate my gratitude to these insightful authors.

In spring of 1995, I sent a one-page summary of the thesis of this book to a select roster of trusted scholars, especially social scientists. I fear the list is too long for enumeration. But at least I want them to know that their candid and careful responses proved to be immensely helpful to me. I hope they find evidence of their contribution in these pages.

Finally, I must testify that I am the lucky beneficiary of the skill and commitment of Michael Leach and his colleagues at Crossroad Herder. It is wonderful to work with publishers who so obviously care about the scholarly and ministerial project of their authors.

Introduction

All authority in heaven and on earth has been given to me. Go therefore and make disciples of all nations.

—Matthew 28:18–19

I BEGAN TEACHING ROMAN CATHOLIC MORAL THEOLOGY IN 1973, almost twenty-five years ago. I imagine that I was not particularly good at it when I began. But I persevered, continued to study, learned from experienced teachers, and eventually, by all accounts I emerged as a skillful practitioner of my craft. I also became a rather demanding teacher, or so my students told me. What I know for myself is that they really learned the visions of moral theology, the riches of the Catholic tradition to which I exposed them.

And it was important to me that they do so. I had entered this field not out of some abstract intellectual curiosity, but because I judged the balanced articulation of Christian morality to be an important, life-nourishing project. (My more cynical friends claimed I was simply coping with the Irish American's typical need to deal with guilt!) And I was teaching ministerial students, whose objective was not only personal understanding but also the ability to use this knowledge in service to others. So I was committed to seeing that they achieved real understanding and usable skill in connecting this wonderful tradition with the everyday needs of people.

And they did. To prove this I have tests successfully passed, presentations and papers admirably constructed, and classroom inter-

1

ventions knowledgeably enacted. You will understand my chagrin, then, when several years later I would listen to them preach as deacons, when I would attend the liturgies they celebrated as newly ordained priests. For the words that came out of their mouths, the visions that they described, bore little resemblance to what they had learned in the classes I had taught.

Little by little I came to a painful realization: whatever else I had achieved in those classes, I had not made contact with those levels of the students where they truly lived. I had not touched the metaphors and images out of which they constructed their personal visions of life. I had not brought them to a point where they would (or could) genuinely embrace the moral perspectives of the best of our tradition and make them their own.

As time went on, I had the occasional opportunity to talk with particular students about this dichotomy. The amazing thing is that they were as confused by it as I was. They would report that they still remembered the insights of our courses, and they still cherished them. When I pointed out the contradiction between those insights and the perspectives presumed by the language of their preaching, they would admit it. And by way of defense, they would simply confess: "I don't know where those words came from. They just came right out of my mouth without intention."

This book was born of that experience.

For perhaps fifteen years I have been exploring the question, Where do people get the values out of which they actually live? Why is it that our efforts at education, no matter how well intentioned, no matter how defensible, achieve so little success? For this is clearly the case. Indeed, as I have taken this question to other settings, this disturbing observation has been often reconfirmed.

Christian leaders have, for these many centuries, been proposing a way of living to which many give lip service. Honesty, fair play, compassion: these are values that many seem to cherish. And yet the data are overwhelming that few in our world live these values consistently. So the question recurs: Why does our teaching so little succeed? Is there no way to find out how people come to choose the values out of which they actually live? And if we could find that out, might we not be more effective in convincing people to live in the humane manner that we wish to sponsor?

This book was born of these questions, and over the last fifteen years I have lived with them, addressing them from first one direction and then another. I have turned to an increasingly wide array of resources in my attempts to shed light. I have encountered many dead ends. But little by little I have also encountered valuable insights. As questions have been replaced slowly by answers, confusion by understanding, this book has struggled toward birth. Now the time has come to share the fruits of my exploration.

Format of the Book

I will engage these questions and lay out my answer through a four-part presentation. In the first part, I will manifest my stubborn streak. Despite my evident failure at "selling to the soul" the best insights of the Catholic moral tradition, I will briefly detail those insights anyway. At the very least, this will allow us to connect what follows to a series of quite traditional notions. At the same time, I hope it will stimulate some admiration for a tradition that is often undervalued.

In the second part, I will present the fruits of extensive research in the social sciences. The explorations that have occupied my attention over the last decade or so have led me to the conclusion that these fields have much to offer us. This is particularly the case with developmental psychology, social psychology, and sociology. For the fact is that the practitioners of these sciences know a good bit about how people come to embrace the values out of which they live. Indeed, in some way this "new question" of mine is an "old question" to them. They are also knowledgeable about the techniques by which we are more likely to contact and perhaps even modify those lived values of particular persons. Through the theoretical explorations of these sciences, and even more through the empirical data of controlled experiments, they have come to a good bit of clarity about which interventions have the greatest likelihood of affecting people's lived values. So I will take the time to detail the results of this research.

The third part will look in another direction. Those who are familiar with contemporary theology will be well aware of the prominent place occupied by "narrative." There have been many books written on "story theology" and on the particular stories that have characterized Christian history. But for all that, I am not aware that anyone has defined clearly the reason why story plays a pivotal role in the shaping—and reshaping—of personal values. That is my project. Utilizing the advances in narrative theory, I will develop a set of strategies for harnessing the power of imagination for the transmission of values.

The fourth part will, at last, apply all of these ideas to the specific projects of ministry. Since issues of application could be explored in an endless series of scenarios, I have needed to limit myself. I have chosen to attempt an application of the insights gleaned from my research to the arenas of religious education, public worship, and parish life. In each case, the perspectives of contemporary theology, social science research, and theories of narrative have been allowed to exercise their influence on pastoral practice.

It should be clear from all this that those who engage in this pastoral practice, ministers of the church, are the primary intended audience for this book. But as I understand it, this group has wide and encompassing membership. First of all, while my roots and commitments are in the Roman Catholic tradition and I give special attention to the theological work of that tradition, my themes are the common possession of all Christians. So I hope that ministers from the various traditions will find these pages welcoming and pertinent. Second, in all these traditions, but particularly in the Catholic world, contemporary events have made us acutely aware that "ministry" is not the possession of the ordained. It is baptism that authorizes one to minister to the sisters and brothers. If the ordained have a particular role, it arises from their special opportunity and particular responsibility to facilitate this common ministerial project. So I am supremely aware that my audience includes all those men and women, baptized all and in some cases vowed or ordained, whose vocation as minister enriches the church on a daily basis.

I know that ministers have a practical bent, given their passion for serving their people. So I will not be surprised if some readers succumb to the temptation to go directly to part 4 of the book. Doing so, I can assure you, will destroy neither your intellectual nor your spiritual life, and it may provide you with some immediately useful ideas. But you will have missed a great deal of practical richness. So my hope is that if you do choose to "cut to the chase," that experience will itself seduce you into returning to the rest of the book.

There you will find food that can nourish your pastoral practice in ways far beyond my meager selection of applications.

Ultimate Goal

For pastoral practice is, in the end, the true focus of this project. In my teaching I have not held as my ultimate interest the mere enrichment of intellectual understanding. I have always been involved in *professional* education. So praxis has been my interest: the mutual interpenetration and enrichment of theory and practice, to the benefit of those one intends to serve. As that has been the focus of my teaching, so it is the focus of this book.

That focus has, itself, determined the title of the book. In one sense, it is a very presumptuous title. Who would dare to accept the project of "making disciples"? Is not this task ultimately in the hands of God? Of course it is. But the opening quotation has emboldened me to accept the title nonetheless. The Gospel of Matthew tells us that Jesus himself gave to his followers the mandate to "make disciples of all nations," so I cannot be accused of having claimed this task for myself or for all ministers on my own authority. I have only embraced what has been presented to us as our sacred duty.

Given that it is our duty, the ultimate sin would be not to do it well. Hence, it becomes clear that the project of this book is also not of my own making. The real reason for the book's importance is not that O'Connell failed to influence his students. Rather, the real reason is that all of us, for lo these many centuries, have too often failed to influence the world. That is a shame. Indeed, that is a scandal. So if the wisdom of the human community can teach us how to do this work more skillfully, should we not open ourselves to learn? Of course we should. And that is why this project is, in my judgment, important indeed.

Making disciples: that is our vocation; that is our responsibility. In God's goodness, may the human insights of this book, joined to the skill and commitment of so many ministers, allow it to happen now as never before.

PART 1

THEOLOGICAL CONTEXT

1

The Shape of Discipleship

THIS IS A BOOK ABOUT MORALITY. MORE SPECIFICALLY, IT IS about moral formation, about the ways in which human persons come to embrace the particular commitments, attitudes, and approaches that shape how they behave. As the book comes to discover how this happens, it will also come to understand how we might be more effective in facilitating the embracing of these life approaches in others.

This is also a book about *Christian* morality, about the ways in which persons come to embrace those ways of living that are characteristically Christian and, consequently, about how we can be more successful in facilitating the embracing of that in others.

But we cannot even engage the question of this book until we have answered a prior question: What do we mean by morality? And more specifically: What do we mean by Christian morality? Addressing these questions will be the object of the first section of the book.

Morality: Human Life Lived Humanely

Sometimes, when one hears people discussing morality, one gets the impression that this reality is something imposed on human persons from the outside. That is, there is an implied presumption that morality is the enemy, beleaguering and burdening me. The suggestion is that if certain people would just stop imposing their demands on me, be that person God, society, or my parents, I could move on with my life without the burden of morality. Then, at last, I could be happy and well adjusted, free at last of the arbitrary demands of these unforgiving voices!

Yet a bit of reflection on our own experience shows that this is not true. The human question What should I do? is an unavoidable part of everyday life. It is a question asked by every human person, unless that person is subject to some sort of serious pathology. It is a question that no normal, mature person can ever avoid.

But let's be clear about the question. What should I do? is a question that can be asked at several different levels. The question can be asked at a "technical" or "procedural" level, with no reference to anything really substantial. That is, we can inquire about how to move most efficiently from here to there, without ever inquiring about whether moving from here to there is worth doing at all. We can wonder how to get the job, how to make the money, how to convince the other person to become intimate, how to conquer the enemy. We can simply take as given that these are worthy objectives for life and then inquire about how best to achieve them. And often enough we do ask this question in that technical way.

But that is not how the question is being understood here. The question What should I do? can also be asked at a deeper level. We can ask: What is the right thing to do? What is the sort of thing a human being ought to do? That is the question we are discussing, and the point being made here is that this deeper, more fundamental question is also a question asked by every normal, mature human being. Sooner or later, people always seem to come to that question. It is not imposed on them from the outside; on the contrary, it seems to arise from the nature of being human.

This does not mean that people always answer the question well. They may answer the question thoughtfully or cavalierly. They may answer it insightfully or naively. Their answers may be distorted by prejudice or ignorance, may be hobbled by pressures of time or limitations of circumstance. But as best I can tell, human persons inevitably ask it.

Consequently, morality is not imposed from the outside, in some arbitrary, posterior, after-the-fact manner. On the contrary, it is built into the fabric of humanity. If all those outside voices were someday to leave us alone, the voice of morality (what is traditionally called the voice of conscience) would be with us still. For the voice is the voice of oneself.

But that is not all; a further point must be made. We human beings are very diverse. We come in various races, various cultures, and two genders. We have greatly diverse views of what life is all about and of what it finally means to be human. So when we ask the question What should I do? we ask it in many different ways. We ask it, indeed, in our own way and in light of who we really are. Consequently, as the question is actually formulated by particular persons, so it is formulated in necessarily diverse ways.

If, for example, I have faith in God, if I believe that God's love has brought me into existence and carries me through every day, then my question will reflect that fact. My question will be: Given God's love for me, what should I do? And if, going further, I have faith in Jesus, if I believe that Jesus Christ is the presence of God in this world, the gift of God to this world, and the one whose loving sacrifice brings us home, then my question will change again. My question will be: Given God and God's gift in Jesus, what should I do?

Christian Morality

This last question, then, brings us to the phenomenon of Christian morality. For Christian morality is nothing more or less than the answer given by Christian persons as they respond to the unavoidable human question in the unavoidably Christian formulation that they give it in their everyday lives. It is the answer given by people who believe in Jesus, as they reflect on their lives, understand those lives in light of the person and deeds of Jesus, and then seek to discern how they ought to act.

In answering their question, however, it is no surprise that Christians depend not only on their experience and their autonomous reflection but also on the words of Jesus. For example, consider the following:

> Just then a lawyer stood up to test Jesus. "Teacher," he said, "what must I do to inherit eternal life?" He said to him, "What is written in the law? What do you read there?" He answered, "You shall love the Lord your God with all your heart, and with all your soul, and with all your strength, and with all your mind; and your neighbor as yourself." And he said to him, "You have given the right answer; do this and you will live." (Luke 19:10–28)[1]

Perhaps no text is more frequently cited in articulating the answer proposed by Christian morality than this. But for that reason, it is worth pointing out that it is a particularly interesting text. Indeed, in a couple of different regards it deserves to be explored.

First of all, it is worth noting that, although the text is usually presented because it is presumed to express *Jesus'* personal "take" on morality, in the text it is not Jesus who gives the answer. It is the lawyer. So at the very least, one must oddly comment that the classic summary of Jesus' view of morality expresses a view that Jesus receives from another, a view he does not articulate but merely affirms.

But if this situation is somehow odd, it is also quite understandable. For, as scholars explain to us, Jesus is not inquiring simplistically into the personal whims of the lawyer. Rather, he is probing in order to assess the lawyer's education. It seems that the answer offered by the lawyer is not, after all, a particularly innovative answer. On the contrary, it is an answer already well accepted in his Jewish community. The "two great commandments," as they are called, are both found in the Hebrew scriptures (Deut. 6:5 and Lev. 19:18); they are not something new with Jesus at all. And, what is more, for generations it had been widely accepted in Jewish culture that all of the commandments of God, and that most traditional of summaries of God's commandments known as the Ten Commandments, could themselves be summarized in the two great commandments: love God and love your neighbor. So in this text, once the lawyer asks Jesus what he must do to inherit eternal life (a question that was perhaps manipulative from the start), Jesus responds with his own question: "Don't you know the commonly accepted answer to the question?" Then the lawyer saves himself by showing that he does, indeed, know that answer: love God and neighbor. Jesus then does nothing more than embrace this tradition and commend it to the lawyer and his other listeners.

So much for distinctively Christian ethics, for a distinctively Christian response to the inevitable human question! Still, if we probe more deeply, this text from Luke is not without innovation. In the following verses the lawyer, "to justify himself," seeks to clarify who the neighbor might be, and Jesus responds with the famous story of the Good Samaritan. That is, in Jesus' view being a neighbor is not a matter of having a relationship or being part of one's group. Quite the contrary, being a neighbor is an attitude of life that should manifest itself in all human encounters.

In this text, and in many others, then, Jesus does articulate something like a characteristically Christian response to the inevitable human question. And what is that response? It is the universalization of the love command.

Discipleship

In the Gospel of Luke, another selection begins almost identically:

> A certain ruler asked him, "Good Teacher, what must I do to inherit eternal life?" Jesus said to him, ". . . You know the commandments. . . ." He replied, "I have kept all these since my youth." When Jesus heard this, he said to him, "There is still one thing lacking. Sell all that you own and distribute the money to the poor, and you will have treasure in heaven; then come, follow me." (Luke 18:18–22)

But if this selection begins like the former one, it ends quite differently. For Jesus' command is not "Love God and neighbor!" Rather it is, "Follow me!" It is the call to the disciple and, by implication, to all persons to be a follower, a disciple of Jesus.

Throughout the pages of the New Testament this scene returns over and over. Indeed, the Greek verb "to follow" (*akoloutheō*) appears ninety-one times. Even more amazing, the Greek noun "disciple" (*mathētēs*) appears 261 times! Clearly, this is a central theme. We are called to be disciples of Jesus. The Christian moral life is a life of discipleship.

But what does it mean to be a follower of Jesus, to live as a disciple? Throughout the pages of the New Testament answers to this question multiply. In one sense, it is a single answer, the very answer that was affirmed in the earlier text analyzed above: love God and neighbor. But in another sense, it is a highly differentiated answer, a multiplicity of situationally pertinent answers. For example, turn to the earliest texts in the New Testament, the letters of St. Paul. There you will discover a predictable pattern. Paul starts his letters with a song of praise, goes on to proclaim the good news of Jesus, and then turns to the challenges that face his readers. And what are those challenges? Often they are understood as the challenge to love; Paul uses that word frequently. But just as often they are quite specific expressions of love, and Paul is not the least bit shy in declaring what he believes to be these specific challenges of discipleship.

The marriage of these two perspectives, the generic and the specific, can be seen in Paul's letter to the Romans. "Let love be genuine; . . . love one another with mutual affection." But just three verses later:

"Contribute to the needs of the saints; extend hospitality to strangers" (12:9–10, 13). If clergy are chastised for joining fundraising to gospel preaching, at least they can point to biblical precedent! Or again, in his first letter to the Corinthians we are blessed with Paul's incomparable paean to love: "If I speak in the tongues of mortals and of angels, but do not have love, I am a noisy gong or a clanging cymbal. . . . And now faith, hope, and love abide, these three; and the greatest of these is love" (13:1, 13). But just pages before, Paul announces, with scarcely less emphasis: "Any man who prays or prophesies with something on his head disgraces his head, but any woman who prays or prophesies with her head unveiled disgraces her head" (11:4–5). Examples could be multiplied: the hortatory generic and the controversial, possibly culture-bound specific are inextricably intertwined.

Similarly adjusted definitions of love's demands are found in the Gospels. It is well known that the text of each of the Gospels, and most particularly each of the Synoptics (Matthew, Mark, and Luke), was focused and nuanced in response to the needs of particular audiences. This focusing is quite evident when we look at explicitations of the challenge of discipleship.

Thus, for example, when the Gospel of Luke presents the Beatitudes, those universally known expressions of discipleship living, the text speaks with simplicity and force about the realities of human suffering: "Blessed are you who are poor. . . . Blessed are you who are hungry" (6:20–21). In the Gospel of Matthew, however, these same Beatitudes evoke a more spiritual perspective, suggesting not the concrete circumstances in which some find themselves but an attitude of life that should characterize all disciples: "Blessed are the poor in spirit. . . . Blessed are those who hunger and thirst for righteousness" (5:3, 6). Similarly, throughout the chapters of the Gospel of Matthew one finds a profound reverence for the Jewish law, not surprising since Matthew was writing to a community of Jewish Christians. In the Gospel of Luke and even more in the letters of Paul, on the contrary, one finds an invitation to be free of that law in order to embrace the focused project of caring for one's neighbor.

What this means is that it is no simple thing to distill the precise shape of discipleship from the pages of the New Testament. The diversity to be found in the New Testament texts themselves is one reason for this. Another is the admitted influence of culture upon the shaping of those texts, as exemplified by the ways in which the perspectives of particular audiences affected the tuning of the texts we have considered above. It is no denial of the fact that Scripture is inspired to admit that the inspiration guides and shapes a culturally limited statement. That is, we can be confident that the Spirit of God assisted the authors and compilers of the New Testament texts and at the same time recognize that these texts were focused on the needs of particular communities. So we are often left with an almost insoluble question: what does this mean for us?

Scripture and Discipleship

Many authors have sought to answer this question. A recent, very refreshing attempt at an answer has been proposed by theologian William Spohn.[2] For Spohn, to be a disciple of Jesus does, indeed, mean that we are meant to learn from him. The role of the disciple is precisely to be a student, benefiting from the gifts of the teacher. But it is not only information that we receive from a teacher. And particularly in the case of Jesus the teacher, it is not information, not concrete moral expectations that we should expect to receive.

Spohn's alternative makes use of an insight from the world of art. How do we learn from a particular painting or drama? It is not that these art works give us specific answers to our daily concerns. But they serve us nonetheless by being "concrete universals." This term, as Spohn develops it, suggests that the work of art is of service precisely because it does not claim to be all things. On the contrary, it is itself, its specific concrete reality. We encounter the work of art in its concreteness. But, paradoxically, by encountering that concreteness, we are able to experience the ways in which it illuminates our experiences, different though they may be.[3]

For Spohn, then, Jesus is the concrete universal for the Christian life. The challenge of the disciple is to experience Jesus in his very concreteness, to experience the teachings of Jesus as these are presented in the New Testament in their concreteness, without asking them to be what they are not. They are culturally situated, and that context cannot help but influence them. But, to the extent that we can experience them in their concreteness, they can illumine our very different settings and give us guidance.

How does this happen? How can we "forgive" the scriptures their culture-bound concreteness and still find them pivotal to defining the shape of discipleship? Spohn specifies three ways in which the reality of Jesus, in his concreteness, can affect us.[4] First, Jesus guides our *per-*

ceptions. So often moral judgments are determined by what we notice or do not notice. The stories of Jesus in the scriptures help us to notice things we might otherwise overlook. Second, the Jesus of the New Testament provides us with profound *motivations.* In morality it is always a very different thing to ask What should I do? than to ask, Why should I do it? The challenge for discipleship that comes from the Jesus of the New Testament is a motivating challenge far more than an instructing challenge, a challenge that energizes perhaps more than it explains. Third, the Jesus of scriptures helps to illumine the disciple's *identity.* By continually speaking of the reality of discipleship, the scriptures tend to shape our identity so that we move into the concrete challenges of everyday life with a self-concept that itself then shapes our consequent behavior.

Scripture, then, plays a pivotal role in shaping Christian morality, in making disciples. But it does not do so by providing one-liners that answer the question, What should I do? Rather, scripture, and in particular the stories of Jesus, serves discipleship by responding to three other questions: What should I see? Why should I act? And who should I be? We will return to all three of these ideas, and especially the relevance of identity to the behaviors of discipleship, in chapter 8.[5]

The Shape of Moral Theology

So the vision of discipleship, as that is presented to us in the pages of scripture, is far more complex than it might appear. This fact helps to explain why, across the centuries, Christians have never ceased to explore the questions around discipleship. They have asked the question, What should I do? And touched by their Christian convictions, they have rephrased that question, What is the challenge of discipleship?

Moral theology, as that term is used in Roman Catholicism, is nothing else than the ongoing project whereby Christians seek to answer the perennial question of discipleship. And since answers to this question are unavoidably complex, it is not surprising that moral theology itself manifests a complex structure. As we proceed with our project, it will prove helpful to us to have seen the general outline of that structure.

First of all, moral theology distinguishes itself into (1) general questions and (2) specific judgments. That is, on the one hand moral theology engages a range of questions that help us understand the overall nature of discipleship. What does it mean to be a moral person? What is the goal of moral decision making? What is it that makes things right and wrong? How shall we understand the activities of the human person as she or he seeks to be moral? How shall we describe the experience of moral weakness and failure?

On the other hand, one can investigate the whole panoply of human interaction, and seek to discover what discipleship means in each particular setting. Thus, for example, one can try to understand the moral requirements of social living. One can seek to discover the nature of well-lived human sexuality. One can ask about the moral ambiguities of conflict, and how to deal with it. One can explore truth telling versus the right to privacy, generosity versus the right to property, the need to interact with others whose values may differ from ours versus the responsibility to be faithful. All of the emerging possibilities of technology can be explored, raising the question as to whether they really serve the project of loving one's neighbor as oneself. And as a daunting example of this issue, one can confront the potential and the limitations of medical science in a world where all eventually die.

Conclusion

Within the first of these two projects, the articulation of general understandings, moral theology posits two subdivisions. As we saw earlier in this chapter, Jesus, quoting the Jewish scriptures, said, "Love your neighbor as yourself." But what does love entail? On the one hand, love is always a matter of good will. That is, the source of love lies in the heart of the human person, where a good intention and a commitment to the good provide the basis for human behavior. On the other hand, in the words of Shakespeare we are called to love both "well" and "wisely." That is, love also involves doing what is truly good for the other person. It is not enough to simply be good of heart. That very goodness of heart should lead to an endeavor of understanding that, in the end, should lead to wisdom. And this wisdom should guide our actions so that the good heart produces helpful acts. Thus, the tradition of Roman Catholic moral theology has distinguished love as benevolence from love as beneficence. What does each of these entail?

Moral theology has addressed the question of beneficence by seeking to understand the nature of right and wrong. What is it that makes behaviors truly right and therefore truly apt expressions of interpersonal love? Moral theology has also sought to understand more deeply love as benevolence. How do the human heart and the human mind work, as they generate a commitment to love in everyday behavior? And, in the end, what shall we say about love that expresses true benevolence but fails to achieve actual beneficence?

In the coming two chapters we will talk in more detail about discipleship viewed from these two perspectives, as rightness of behavior and as commitment of heart. We shall try to understand the traditional ways in which Roman Catholic moral theology has engaged the question of discipleship from these two perspectives. The next chapter will unveil beneficence, while the following will focus on benevolence. Finally, as we conclude part 1 we will come to see the deficiencies in these traditional responses and some new theological possibilities being explored today.

The statement of these possibilities will set the stage for the major investigation of this book, the making of disciples.

Notes

1. Pope John Paul II uses this text, in its Matthean version (19:16–22), as the basis for a meditation on the nature of morality; see "Veritatis Splendor," *Origins* 23:18 (October 14, 1993): §§6–27.

2. William Spohn, *What Are They Saying About Scripture and Ethics*, revised (New York: Paulist Press, 1995). Chapter 5, where Spohn offers his constructive statement, presents these arguments. He first outlined this approach in "Jesus and Ethics," *Catholic Theological Society of America Proceedings* 49 (1994): 40–57.

3. Spohn, *What Are They Saying*, 99. In developing this idea, Spohn acknowledges his dependence on literary scholar William Wimsatt, *The Verbal Icon: Studies in the Meaning of Poetry* (Lexington: University of Kentucky Press, 1954), 71.

4. Spohn, *What Are They Saying*, 102.

5. This view of the way scripture influences Christian ethics is also held—and articulately explained—by Lisa Sowle Cahill, "Moral Methodology: A Case Study," *Chicago Studies* 19 (1980): 171–88.

2

Objective Discipleship

EVER SINCE THE CALL OF JESUS, CHRISTIANS HAVE STRUGGLED to clarify the challenge of discipleship. As they sought to convert their souls so as to embrace discipleship more fully, they simultaneously also worked to clarify their minds so that they could understand the shape of that discipleship more fully. As this project continued over the centuries, certain ways of expressing the matter began to become conventional. They were found to catch the truth in a particularly helpful way.

This process of developing a systematic approach to the discussion of discipleship came to be known as moral theology. Thus, in one sense we can say that moral theology has existed as long as followers of Jesus have struggled to understand truly the shape of discipleship. But for most of our religious history, the term "moral theology" would not have been used. Rather, this project of understanding discipleship was integrated into the larger project of understanding the reality of Jesus and his mission and of the God from whom that Jesus came. Thus, the project would simply have been called "theology" and would have included both dogmatic and ethical elements, authentically interwoven.

This changed in the period after the Protestant Reformation. In the course of developing its response to the Reformation, the Catholic Church convened an ecumenical council, the Council of Trent (1545–1563). The Council in turn mandated a massive restructuring of programs for the preparation of clergy, to deal with some of the abuses Luther and other Reformers had condemned. Thus, seminaries were born, schools whose sole purpose was to produce dependable and consistently educated clergy. Seminaries were to be intellectually respectable. But perhaps more important, they were to ensure that all ordained clergy were aware of reasonable, moderate, and acceptable positions on the questions of the day. In service to that objective, a collection of textbooks was developed over about two hundred years. These textbooks, the manuals, were a particular creation of the seminary project, summarizing moderate, perhaps "conventional," positions on the whole range of theological questions. Finally, and not surprisingly, when the curricula for seminaries were detailed, special emphasis was given to right behavior. Thus, three "new" sciences appeared: canon law, liturgics, and moral theology, proposing right behavior in church life, in worship, and in general human affairs, respectively. These sciences were not new because their questions were novel, of course. Rather, they were new because their format, pursuing isolated discussions separated from broader theological considerations, was unprecedented.

Outline of the Manuals

The manuals of moral theology became quite consistent in the way they addressed the core questions of discipleship. Eventually their approach became paradigmatic and has remained so until recently. It will serve our reflections to become familiar with that approach.

When one considers the question What is discipleship? it becomes clear that two subsidiary questions are implied. On the one hand, What is the objective of discipleship? And on the other hand, What is the look of the disciple?

The first question became the starting point for an overarching theory of objective morality. What is right and wrong? What makes behavior correct? What is the shape of moral obligation? What can be said about laws, divine and human? Questions such as these were engaged as part of the first focus of the moral manuals.

The second focus, instead of looking outward at the "moral world," looked inward at the "moral person." Here there was a different set of questions. How shall we understand the challenge to personal authenticity? What is required for a person to be genuinely responsible for his or her choices? What is the shape of good choices? What does it mean to speak of sin as the scriptures and tradition always have? In what sense can we speak of conscience, its dictates, and its obligations? Questions such as these constituted the second focus of the moral manuals.

Since our goal is to understand more fully how to develop in ourselves and in others the life of discipleship, we are in some ways taking a new look at these same traditional questions. Thus, even though we will eventually go well beyond traditional answers to these questions, looking indeed to a completely different source for the wisdom we seek, it will prove to be important that we have taken a few moments to situate ourselves in this ancient conversation. In this chapter and the next, therefore, we will reprise in the briefest manner the vision of discipleship that comes to us from the tradition of Catholic moral theology and was transmitted through the centuries of moral manuals.[1]

We begin, then, with the first of the great questions of moral theology: What is the nature of right and wrong? Or to put this another way: When we set out to make a moral judgment, what is our goal? What makes a moral judgment *right* judgment? Is there such a thing as "objective morality"? And if there is, how can we understand it?

Objective Values

You will not be surprised to learn that the Catholic tradition affirmed quite forcefully the existence of objective morality. What may prove a bit more interesting is how that morality was understood. When the manualist tradition spoke about objective morality, it routinely focused on the "natural law," which is a philosophical term inherited from the ancient Greeks. But since that term is subject to so many distortions, we will use a different nomenclature. In the twentieth century, the core convictions of the tradition have come to be expressed in the language of "values." That is to say, realizing the reality of objective morality involves realizing the reality of objective values, values not created by human whim but preexisting human insight. Values are to be noticed, observed, appreciated, embraced, and honored. They are not, in this conception, to be created.

The understanding of values that comes out of this Catholic tradition can be amplified if we consider four declarations about values. First, they are real. Second, they are affected by our world's finite reality. Third, they are susceptible to change across space and time. And fourth, they are rooted in the dignity of human persons. Let's look at each of these in turn.

First of all, values are *real*. That is, as has already been mentioned, they are not created by human intention. Rather, they are discovered. The Catholic tradition spoke endlessly about this prior reality of objective moral values. In so doing, it was proclaiming its rejection of two counterfeit visions of morality.

The first counterfeit rejected by the tradition in favor of a vision of objective morality was *relativism*. Relativism asserts that the only true value is the sincerity and authenticity of the moral agent. "The only important thing is that you be sincere in whatever you do." Thus, for the relativist any particular action, no matter what its objective appearance, would be morally right if it comes from a sincere intention. Behavior does not, in and of itself, have value that needs to be honored.[2]

Relativism has, of course, presented itself in various guises over the centuries. Fourteenth-century nominalism was a version of the relativistic perspective. European existentialism in the early part of the twentieth century deserves that name, as does the situation ethics of Joseph Fletcher and others.[3] Some have argued that the civil philosophy of the United States is intrinsically relativistic, since it lays such high store upon individual dignity and respect for individual choice.[4]

Over and over again through the centuries, from the writings of Thomas Aquinas to the encyclicals of John Paul II, Catholic moral theology has opposed relativism.[5] It has consistently claimed that there is a "real world" that is not infinitely malleable to human intention. Behavior has value in and of itself and not simply because it is enacted by a subjectively sincere agent. Thus, to ask the question: Did you mean well? is to ask only the first question. A second question must also follow: Was the action you elected to perform truly the right one?

If relativism is a seductive counterfeit alternative to the objective moral vision of the Catholic tradition, it is not the only counterfeit. Equally at variance with that tradition is a *legalism* that understands morality to be a simple matter of conforming to existing law. Legalism claims that behaviors are wrong because they are prohibited, rather than the other way around. Consequently, the legalist looks outward to various seats of authority to determine what ought to be done.[6]

One can distinguish various sorts of legalists. The civil legalist naively equates morality with good citizenship, presuming that whatever legitimate government requires is the good to be done. In Catholic circles one often encounters the ecclesiastical legalist, the person who understands morality as obedience to church legislation in such a way that the legislation is understood as itself making something right or wrong. And then there is the legalism of the fundamentalist, the one who believes that actions are right or wrong depending on some arbitrary decision of God which is to be found in the Bible or in some other text.

Ironically, legalists share with relativists the central conviction that behavior has no meaning in and of itself. They simply enact that conviction in different ways. The relativist responds with an exaggerated assertion of personal autonomy. The legalist responds with an abject subjugation to exterior authority. In a strange sort of way, a legalist can be understood as an alienated relativist. Conversely, a relativist is one committed to a legalism in which the self is the only legitimate authority.

At its best, the Catholic tradition has resisted both of the seductive counterfeits. To be candid, it has been more successful in fighting relativism than it has in avoiding legalism. For various historical and political reasons, church teaching on moral matters has often walked the thin edge of legalism, so emphasizing the rights of legitimate teaching authority that the center of moral value in the significance of the act itself is sometimes lost. This is, as I have suggested, ironic. For to the extent that the church has allowed at least the appearance of legalism to exist, it has actually fallen victim to that very relativism which it so forcefully rejects.

In contrast to both of these seductive counterfeits, however, the core of the natural law tradition has continued to assert the intrinsic significance of objective behavior. Acts are good or bad not because they are approved or prohibited and also not because they are personally satisfying or repugnant but because they are genuinely worthy of and in service to humanity in a good world. To the extent that behavior has this shape and this effect, it is morally right. To the extent that behavior is otherwise, it is morally wrong.

In a Real World

The real values asserted by this Catholic tradition exist in a real world. But the world has two characteristics that are themselves inescapable. And because they are inescapable, they affect the way in which values exist.

For one thing, it is a *finite* world. That is to say, it is a world in which a person may be able to do "anything," but most certainly cannot do "everything." To be here is not to be there. To spend money on this is to not have money to spend on that. To make this choice is to let go of that choice. In a finite world everything "costs," and there is no way of avoiding this.

The implication of this worldly finitude is that moral choices always involve trade-offs. A common colloquialism would say that morality offers the challenge to "do good and avoid evil." It is more accurate, however, to say that morality demands that one do "as much good as possible and as little evil as necessary." That is, right moral behavior involves doing that which is truly good in a world where one cannot do all goods. Or, to put this another way, *moral* evil occurs where one behaves in a manner unnecessarily (and therefore unacceptably) destructive.

This was the understanding of the tradition when it declared that the virtue perhaps most necessary to the moral person is prudence. That is, in order to live a right moral life one needs the skill of discerning what is the best of the available options in a complex and ambiguous world. Similarly, the tradition often spoke with reverence of the need for a "proportionate reason" for the toleration of unavoidable evil. That is, even in a finite world, one should not allow evil to take place without good reason. And that good reason is not just a subjectively good reason (relativism) but an objectively good reason, a proportionate reason. The fact that the good truly and objectively outweighs the evil being done is precisely what makes an act the morally right choice.[7]

The second thing about this world is that it is a place of *variety* and *change,* a place of time and space. And these factors also affect objective values.

Values exist in space. That is to say, what is truly, objectively good in one place may not be so in another place. As one wag once put it, morally appropriate attire is quite different on a beach than it is in a cathedral (even though in Chicago, for example, these locations are only a few blocks apart). This is not to say that behavior is relativistic, in the sense that its moral character is subject to the whim of the agent. It is simply to say that objective context changes from place to place. It may be moral to shoot one's gun in the midst of a farm field. It would not be moral to do the same thing on a downtown city street. What is morally upright, because genuinely worthy of and helpful to human persons, may be different in Latin America than it is in the countries of Asia. Objective morality is nonetheless also situated morality, and thus good moral judgment needs always to be attentive to the true facts of the particular case in the actual situation.

In the same way, the true world is a world of time. Even the objective world changes. Thus, behavior that was genuinely good because genuinely helpful at one time may not necessarily be so at another time. This is obviously true in the case of the various moments of a particular person's life. Sexual behavior that is wrong for the unmarried becomes right when one marries; the change involved in marital commitment is not accidental, it is substantial. It is also true in the case of the moments in the life of the human family. There are, for example, those who argue that capital punishment may once have been genuinely helpful, perhaps even necessary, to the humanizing of the human community, but is no longer so. Others make the same claim as regards war. A long string of Roman Catholic popes has pointed out a change in the nature of private property, from a time when it was totally private, that is to say, totally under the control of its owner, to a time when it has an "intrinsically social function." Now even private property must serve the commonweal, at least by being utilized in a way that is sensitive to those common needs. One is less the "owner" of one's property than one is its "steward."

Thus, the objective of discipleship is to do what is truly right. And what is right is that which is truly good, truly worthy of human persons and helpful to them. But what is truly good is always truly good in a particular (objective) context. It is truly and objectively good, given the alternatives actually available and in the here and now that actually exists.

Created World

But if the pursuit of real values must take place in a world that is real, it must also take place in a world that is created. That is, in the view of this Catholic tradition, the world is always understood as coming from the hand of a loving and caring God. Thus, the world is not morally neutral. Even less is it morally evil. Rather, the world is good, in some ways sacred. And in a very particular fashion, the human person is intrinsically good, in some ways even sacred. Thus, this moral vision of real values is based on the intrinsic, nonnegotiable dignity of human persons.

Various scholars have described this dignity in various ways. Some have said that reflection upon the human person reveals a series of basic goods, so intrinsic to what it means to be human that attacking those basic goods always constitutes an attack upon the good of the human person. Thus, at any place and at any time, a direct attack on these basic goods would always be immoral. [8] Others have preferred to say that reverence for the sacredness of the human person demands a never-ending project of discerning the best that is possible in serving that person. In any case, the nonnegotiable dignity of the human persons, not rooted in the person's intelligence or utility or beauty or productivity, but rather rooted in the very created reality of the human person, is the foundation of the Catholic vision of objective morality.

One can say, then, that the very paradigm of wrong moral behavior is behavior that betrays the identity of the human person or violates the intrinsic dignity of that person. And understanding that persons never live alone but always in the context of community, one can also argue that the direct undermining of the reality of human relationships and communities is likewise intrinsically immoral.

Conclusion

This Catholic vision of morality, then, throughout the many centuries of its development, has remained true to a few core insights. In opposition both to relativism and to legalism it has held the notion that discipleship involves attention to objective preexisting values. The values are real, the creation neither of the whim of the agent nor of the will of the legislator. These real values exist, however, in a world of finitude, of space and of time, a world where neither conflict nor change can be avoided. The skill of prudence, consequently, remains pivotal as one seeks to discern what is the best thing to do. The fundamental foundation on which that discernment process builds is the understanding that this objective world which confronts me, the disciple, is a world that itself comes from the hand of God. It is a world that participates in divinity in a mysterious but genuine way. It is a world that is characterized by dignity and worth that are nonnegotiable. Thus, the real world calls for acknowledgment, affirmation, and respect. It also, in some deeper way, calls for a posture of reverence.

In some ways, this *reverence for the real* is at the heart of discipleship.

Notes

1. This author has contributed directly to this traditional conversation about moral theology in his *Principles for a Catholic Morality*, revised edition (San Francisco: Harper & Row, 1990). The synthetic presentation of the tradition that follows is derived from that book. Those wishing to pursue these

questions in greater detail can confer that work as well as Richard Gula's splendid book *Reason Informed by Faith* (New York: Paulist Press, 1989).

2. Relativism seems to be a perennially seductive counterfeit vision of morality. In a recent speech, Cardinal Joseph Ratzinger, a recognized theologian and the leader of the Vatican's Congregation for the Doctrine of the Faith (the office charged with protecting Catholic orthodoxy), has argued that relativism is the gravest threat to Catholic morality in our time ("Relativism: The Central Problem for Faith Today," *Origins* 26:20 [October 31, 1996]: 309–17).

3. Joseph Fletcher, *Situation Ethics: The New Morality* (Philadelphia: Westminster Press, 1966).

4. See, e.g., Robert Bellah et al., *Habits of the Heart: Individualism and Commitment in American Life* (Berkeley: University of California Press, 1985).

5. See, e.g., Pope John Paul II's encyclical "Veritatis Splendor" (*Origins* 32:18 [October 14, 1993]): "man's capacity to know the truth is also darkened, and his will to submit to it is weakened. Thus, giving himself over to relativism and skepticism . . . , he goes off in search of an illusory freedom apart from truth itself" (§4).

6. It is because it smacks of legalism that we are avoiding the term "natural law." Actually, the tradition was quite clear that natural law is law of a quite different sort. A typical formulation would have declared that if natural law is truly "law," then at least it is law promulgated in the very act of creation! In other words, it is a law that makes certain things wrong not by edict but by constructing reality in such a way that they truly are wrong (i.e., harmful or destructive).

7. A question occurs at this point: Are there some behavioral choices that are *always and intrinsically* immoral? About this question there are strenuous debates that cannot detain us here. Suffice it to say that if there are such acts (as this author claims there are), the reason they are such is precisely because in all circumstances they are either disproportionately destructive or directly antithetical to the moral project of caring for the neighbor. For a full explanation of this position, see *Principles for a Catholic Morality*, revised edition, 202–14.

8. This way of speaking is associated primarily with philosopher Germain Grisez, e.g., *The Way of the Lord Jesus* (Chicago: Franciscan Herald Press, 1983). See also John Finnis, *Fundamentals of Ethics* (Washington, D.C.: Georgetown University Press, 1983).

3

The Look of the Disciple

IF WE ARE GOING TO ACHIEVE AN ENRICHED UNDERSTANDING
of the dynamics by which a life-style of discipleship is developed within
human persons, and on that basis a clearer strategy for encouraging
people to embrace the life of discipleship, one of our needs is a clear
understanding of personhood itself. The tradition of Roman Catholic
moral theology gave considerable attention to describing the moral
person. We shall eventually discover that this traditional description
was in some ways flawed. Indeed, these flaws in the description of the
moral person in large part account for our inability to be effective in
facilitating the process of discipleship, as we shall see. Thus, we will
need to complete a "traditional" view of the person by an "enriched"
one. Nonetheless, it is important to start from the basis of that traditional understanding. This chapter will be devoted to laying it out in
some detail.

In the schema developed in medieval philosophy and manifest in
the manuals of Roman Catholic moral theology, what is important
about the human person is that she or he is characterized by knowledge and freedom. It is these two qualities, capacities, and activities
that make moral decision making possible. To understand knowledge
and freedom, then, is to understand how the person operates as a
moral agent. Or to put this another way, to understand knowledge and
freedom is to understand the activities whereby discipleship is
embraced.

There is nothing particularly surprising in this insight. It is the common heritage of philosophy in the medieval and modern period. So,

for our purposes there is no need to belabor it. But it will be helpful to say a few things and, in particular, to notice in each case one significant development to be found already present within the theological tradition itself, developments that provide an entrée into the more enriched contemporary understanding of the moral person, to which we shall later turn.

Knowledge

With regard to human knowing, it became commonplace in the Roman Catholic moral tradition to speak of two different kinds of knowing. On the one hand, there is mere "speculative" knowledge, *cognitio speculativa*. That is to say, there is information that a person has or receives, information that the person *happens* to possess but that is in no way *important* to him or her. Thus, a person may have a speculative understanding of the theory of relativity or the existence of nine Beethoven symphonies. Indeed, one may even have a speculative understanding of the value of telling the truth!

On the other hand, there is another sort of knowledge, "evaluative" knowledge. Some of the manuals of moral theology written in Latin denominated this second kind of knowledge as *cognitio aestimativa*.[1] That is to say, it is knowledge that involves an estimation or appreciation of the value involved. It is a genuine, appropriated, integrated knowledge. It is a knowledge that a person owns in a personally significant way. The fact that my spouse loves me, for example, is a fact of which I have evaluative and not merely speculative knowledge.

Please note that the difference between these two sorts of knowledge is not a difference in the thing known. For the highly educated scientist, for example, it is quite possible that $e = mc^2$ may carry deeply felt significance. Similarly, the fact that your spouse cares for you may simply be a matter of speculative knowledge to me. So the difference between speculative and evaluative knowledge lies not in what is known but rather in the way the thing is known by the knower.

Manuals of moral theology, for example that of Josef Fuchs, were bold in declaring that for a genuinely human moral act nothing less than evaluative knowledge will suffice.[2] True moral obligation does not arise from the bare facts of information; rather, moral obligation arises from the "felt" awareness of particular moral obligations. This is a surprising declaration. Facile accounts of moral obligation often seem to suggest that we can generate in other people a true obligation by the mere recitation of the facts of moral duty. That, however, was not the teaching of the Catholic moral tradition.

A somewhat similar insight was articulated by Cardinal John Henry Newman, the famous nineteenth-century English convert. In explaining the nature of conscience, and of the faith that was its basis, Newman made a clear distinction between "notional assent" and "real assent."[3] Only the latter, an assent rooted in both intellect and feeling, could serve as the basis for the true obligation of the believer. Simply because human beings have particular items of information, it does not follow that they actually understand and appreciate what is at stake. Consequently, it is not to be presumed that they will actually live out of this knowledge. Nor will it constitute a genuinely human decision if they happen to act in contradiction of that information.

Philosopher Jacques Maritain similarly sensed the unity of the human person when he described "connatural knowledge" as distinct from dry intellectual knowledge. In a passage filled with pertinence to our project, Maritain declared:

> I used a moment ago the expression "knowledge through connaturality." It refers to a basic distinction made by Thomas Aquinas, when he explains that there are two different ways to judge of things pertaining to a moral virtue, say fortitude. On the one hand, we can possess in our mind moral science, the conceptual and rational knowledge of virtues, which produces in us a merely intellectual conformity with the truths involved. . . .
>
> On the other hand, we can possess the virtue in question in our own powers of will and desire, have it embodied in ourselves, and thus be in accordance with it or connatured with it in our very being. . . .
>
> This particular kind of knowledge through connaturality comes about, I think, by means of emotion.[4]

The point is that although human beings know many things in this manner, in an abstract, speculative, uninvolved fashion, such a knowing is not an adequate basis for moral living. Human beings do not, in fact, live out of mere items of information which they happen to possess. Rather, the sort of knowing that one observes when human beings make moral choices and enact moral commitments is a different sort, a sort called "evaluative" knowing.

Freedom

In the second place, said the tradition, the moral person is characterized by freedom. It is almost jejune to declare that moral choice

involves choice! But if this is true, then it follows that moral action pre-
supposes the ability freely to choose. Consequently, the capacity for
discipleship resides in human persons precisely because, and to the
extent that, these persons are genuinely free. And this was, indeed, the
consistent claim of the tradition. But for all its self-evidence, this
human characteristic of freedom has received important and careful
reflection. And again in this case, a review of recent articulations of
the tradition reveals an intriguing extension of customary claims.

The school of theology known as "transcendental Thomism," most
particularly as this was articulated by German theologian Karl Rahner,
makes much of the fact that the human person is a multileveled being.
There are more "superficial" levels of the human person wherein the
person acts, makes ordinary day-to-day choices, and reflects on experience. Because these levels of the human person engage the ordinary
categories of experience, they are described as "categorical." To put
this another way, ordinary human behaviors, including human decision making, exemplify human activity at the categorical level.

But the human person has deeper levels, levels that underlie and
support ordinary behavior and day-to-day activity but are not identical
with them. These deeper levels are manifested through everyday
human behavior, and conversely they make everyday human behavior
genuinely meaningful. These deeper levels of the human person are
more abiding, less subject to change, more slowly developed, and
therefore in some ways more fully expressive of the personhood of the
agent. Because these deeper levels transcend any particular item of
everyday behavior, they can be described as "transcendental."

This insight of Rahner and his colleagues, that human behavior and
human freedom involve both transcendental and categorical levels, is
really very simple at its core. It is an attempt to notice that, in the case
of human persons, the everyday behavior that one observes does not
exhaust the reality of the being. We are, quite literally, more than our
individual acts. We are never apart from our individual acts, of course;
but we are not exhausted by those acts, either. Beneath our individual
acts there is an abiding personhood. This personhood is manifested by
the acts and, since the relationship between the categorical and transcendental levels is reciprocal, is also influenced by those acts. But the
personhood is also more than the acts.

In recent decades, this insight into the deeper dimensions of the
human person has generated a number of new ways of describing the
moral world. On the American scene, the first inkling of this perspec-

tive to strike most Catholics was provided by a proposal that, beneath everyday behavior, the moral person is characterized by a "fundamental option." The point of this term, the insight in whose service it was coined, was simply that within the human person there exist abiding postures, expressed in behavior and shaped by behavior but always more than behavior. However, since this newly coined term was "option," there was a tendency for people to view it over against everyday behavior, as if it was one more choice next to other human choices. The understanding of fundamental option consequently became caricatured: people went home and tried to make one![5]

This led to the choice on the part of some theologians to speak instead of a "fundamental stance."[6] Thus, everyday options, behaviors in which moral choice takes place, exert influence on, while they are also expressive of, the basic stance of a person's life. Even more recently, with the growing appreciation for the movements of human development, there has been a tendency to speak of "fundamental direction."[7] Whichever terminology proves to be the most useful, the core insight has been an abiding part of Roman Catholic moral theology for over a half century. And what is that core insight? It is that, in the case of human beings, behavior does not exhaust the reality of the being. Rather, in addition to the individual acts, there is the abiding shape of the freely chosen identity of the person. And this abiding, underlying transcendental shape, mutually interacting with concrete categorical choices, is of pivotal importance in defining the moral reality of human life, the inner dynamism of the life of discipleship.

Impediments

One last set of ideas should be added here, in order that this brief summary of the traditional understanding of the moral person may serve us well as we undertake our contemporary project of defining how to help in making disciples.

It is not unusual for commentators in the field of moral philosophy to ridicule the Scholastic vision of the human person, with its focus on knowledge and freedom as key elements, by claiming that is it simplistic, that it ignores the complexity of the human person. To some extent this criticism is warranted, but not entirely so. The vision of the human person developed by this moral tradition, even in its older incarnations, was more sophisticated than it would appear at first glance. And the idea that introduced this note of subtlety into the scheme was the idea of "impediments."[8] As we have seen, human persons, in the pursuit of their moral activity, are characterized by knowledge and freedom. But the human's possession of knowledge and freedom, at any given moment and even in the whole course of a lifetime, is profoundly affected by a variety of impediments, factors resisting the dynamics of knowing and choosing.

In the case of that sort of evaluative knowledge which is the necessary substratum of authentic moral choice, the most obvious impediment is ignorance itself. And the tradition was explicitly aware of the many faces of ignorance. There is, first of all, a very simple absence of information. Beyond that, there is the absence of a proper appreciation of the significance of particular pieces of information. Indeed, the abiding difficulty of transforming speculative knowledge into evaluative knowledge is itself an example of this ignorance, which impedes proper moral choice.

To the obvious impediment of ignorance, the tradition added three more, all of which have in common that they affect both knowledge and freedom: passion, force, and fear. The language, of course, is rather quaint, but the insight is not. *Passion* refers to the fact that out-of-control emotions can get in the way of good moral judgment. This assertion of the tradition reveals an abiding suspicion of the role of emotion, a suspicion that will demand our attention later in this book.[9] But even those who appreciate the positive role of emotion will also recognize the ways in which it can undermine genuine human behavior. *Force* refers to actual compulsion from outside the person. If I tie you down, I get in the way of your free choice! *Fear,* on the other hand, refers to control that comes from within. Perhaps this is a subset of the category "passion," but the tradition was particularly sensitive to the way in which fear gets in the way of free choice. If anything, our modern experience confirms that insight, as therapists help clients find release from paralyzing fear.

These four impediments, ignorance, passion, force, and fear, have in common the fact that they tend to be associated with particular moments in a person's life. And in principle at least, all four are able to be transcended through additional effort. The tradition also spoke of four impediments that are less easily transcended, since they are characteristics of the very personhood of the moral agent. These four "habitual impediments" are personality, habits, false opinion, and mental illness.

To claim that one's personality is itself an impediment is rather ironic; yet it is also a datum of human experience. People talk comfortably about being either "morning persons" or "evening persons," and contemporary psychology has done much to remind people that there are various personal types and temperaments. Habits that are ingrained in a particular person similarly exercise an influence over human choice. There was a tendency in the tradition to view habits as impeding authentic human choice. As we shall see in the next chapter, it is also possible to understand them as facilitating that choice. Still, no one would deny that one of the challenges of human life is dealing with one's "bad habits."

Third, the tradition described an abiding impediment that it called "false opinions." The reality would be more easily recognized in our time by the term "prejudice." It is more than mere ignorance, which we discussed above. It is a sort of counterfeit knowledge, a misunderstanding that actively prevents the acquisition of accurate knowledge. We so often see just what we expect to see in ambiguous circumstances. To the extent that our past experience has led us to anticipate certain patterns of behavior—for example, critical responses to our ideas—we will see them even when they are not present. Thus, prejudice can systematically erode the attempt to authentically live out the moral life. Finally, even the "primitive" perspective of medieval moral theology recognized that mental illness gets in the way of mature human living. How much more we know about this truth today!

In sum, the Roman Catholic tradition of moral theology understood the human person as characterized by knowledge and freedom, and at the same time recognized that the achievement of knowledge and freedom is a lifelong, tortuous project. Impediments, both occasional and abiding, constitute blocks to the achievement of this genuinely human project.

Culpability

This vision of the human person was exemplified in the tradition's discussion of sin, and particularly of culpability. Since the nuanced and precise meaning of these terms was often lost in popular presentations, it will be worth a brief comment.

The term "culpability" is generally used to describe personal responsibility with regard to specific moral actions. The question would be asked: Is the person actually culpable for the (presumably wrong) moral choice that has been made? Did the person really commit sin in performing this act? The response might then be given that even though an act had taken place that was in many ways characteristically human, some lack of the requisite knowledge or freedom meant that true culpability was lacking. For a person can be considered personally culpable for an act only when genuine evaluative knowledge is present and true human freedom expressed. Only then can it be said that the person has committed sin.

One must candidly admit that this vision was not always maintained in pastoral practice. For example, it was common to name specific acts and declare that such and such "is a mortal sin." Of course, there is no way in which an individual act can be described unequivocally as being a sin. Sin, that is to say, genuinely culpable human behavior, depends on the conditions of knowledge and freedom. To be precise, the statement in question was really declaring that such and such is a wrong thing to do and that anyone who does it knowingly and freely will be committing a sin, that is, will be performing an authentically culpable human act. But such careful language has not always been reverenced.

Still, if casual conversation often neglected the complexities involved in human culpability, the best of the tradition, at least when formally taught, did not. And that is a consolation as we attempt to appreciate the full richness of the shape of human discipleship.

Conscience

In the last chapter we discussed the abiding commitment of the Roman Catholic tradition to the reality of objective morality. In this chapter we have focused on that tradition's understanding of the human person and of the critical role of personal authenticity. It is in the tradition's discussion of conscience that these two perspectives are most decisively and ingeniously blended.

The notion of conscience derives from secular philosophy, most anciently in the writings of the Greek Stoics. It enters Christian theology in the writings of St. Paul, particularly in his first letter to the Corinthians. After that, it is never entirely absent from the theological conversation. It is discussed at length by Thomas Aquinas, and then in the manual tradition of the Counter-Reformation it achieves a classic formulation.

In this formulation, the word "conscience" is seen as pointing at three distinct facets of the human person. In traditional moral theology, these were known, respectively, as *synderesis, moral science,* and

syneidesis. More simply, I have referred to them as conscience/1, con-
science/2, conscience/3.[10]

The word "conscience," in the first place, is used to point at an abiding dimension of human personhood. That dimension is the radical
sense of personal responsibility. Some have argued that this sense of
responsibility is always present in human beings unless they are profoundly flawed by mental illness. Others, less sanguinely, understand
the sense of responsibility as a capacity, a potential easily derailed by
poor upbringing and needing cultivation, perhaps even training. In
any case, the fundamental basis for moral activity is the abiding sense
on the part of the moral agent that she or he is responsible for decisions and behavior. This abiding sense of responsibility deserves the
name "conscience," what we may call conscience/1.

The two other dimensions of the human person that the tradition
understood as conscience both build on the foundation of con-
science/1. But they relate differently, on the one hand toward the
objective reality of natural law, and on the other hand toward the subjective reality of personal authenticity.

One can say that, precisely because the human person is responsible
for decision and behavior, the human person unavoidably sets out on
the project of trying to discover what ought to be done. Thus, "conscience" can be used to point at the human process whereby a person
seeks to discern what is the right thing to do. This process of discernment is ongoing: sometimes it lasts mere seconds; sometimes it lasts
for years. In any case, it is a process to which the person feels committed precisely because of that fundamental sense of accountability (con-
science/1). And what is the goal of that process? The goal, of course,
is to discover what truly, objectively ought to be done. Thus, in some
ways in the activity of conscience/2 the true focus is not conscience
but rather the natural law. That is, the activity of conscience/2 represents the human person's pilgrimage in search of objective moral
truth. In this context, then, one would not speak of the "rights" of conscience. Quite the contrary, one has an acute sense of the "duties of
conscience."

The ongoing project of discernment cannot, however, last forever.
Sooner or later, the exigencies of life demand that one act. To act in a
humanly appropriate fashion, however, is to freely decide, and decision
is possible only on the basis of judgment. So there comes a moment in
which the human person must conclude the process of ongoing discernment, draw its reflections together, and allow them to issue in a

judgment: "As best I can tell, I ought to do X." At this moment, then, "conscience" describes an act. But not an act of external behavior; rather an internal act of personal judgment. The person judges, on the best available information achieved by the process of conscience/2, that a particular behavioral choice is the right one to do. This judgment is itself an act of conscience, conscience/3.

But since conscience/1 asserts that it is central to human identity that one be responsible for one's behavior, it follows that this personal judgment takes on the character of a command. What I believe I ought to do, I experience myself as commanded to do. Thus the act of conscience/3, the decisive judgment by which the person affirms what ought to be done, becomes a demanding guide for personal moral behavior. To conform one's behavior to that personal judgment is, by definition, sanctity. To choose, instead, to contravene that personal judgment is sin.

This personal act of judgment (conscience/3) is not capricious, of course, since it is nothing else than the current summary of insights gleaned through the very humble process of discernment that we call conscience/2. At the same time, it is usually not absolutely certain either. For the process of discernment almost always suggests that, with more time and more resources, one might learn more. There is a paradox here, then. The personal judgment is, unavoidably, somehow tentative. It is nonetheless experienced as compelling.

Conclusion

Thus, understood in this way, conscience holds up in bold relief the identity of the moral subject challenged to authenticity, called upon to live out of knowledge and freedom, understanding culpability as identical with internal choice and not with accidents of external behavior. This vision of conscience, then, pulls together the twin focuses of natural law and personal autonomy. Or perhaps it might be better to say, this vision of conscience takes that tension and brings it into a narrow focus, replicating that universal tension in a tension within the human person.

The understanding of conscience presented by the Roman Catholic moral tradition, then, both summarizes and clarifies the overall vision of morality that we have presented in the last two chapters. Both the external objective of discipleship and the internal shape of discipleship are manifest in this traditional vision. The theology of conscience appropriately brings to a conclusion the summary that these two chapters have pursued.

Notes

1. E.g., Josef Fuchs, *Theologia Moralis Generalis* I (Rome: Editrice Università Gregoriana, 1960), 155. I first learned this distinction between *cognitio speculativa* and *cognitio aestimativa* from Fuchs's work.

2. See also my discussion of this notion in *Principles for a Catholic Morality*, revised edition (San Francisco: Harper & Row, 1990), 58–63.

3. John Henry Cardinal Newman, *The Grammar of Assent* (Notre Dame, Ind.: University of Notre Dame Press, 1979), 49–92.

4. Jacques Maritain, *A Maritain Reader* (Garden City, N.Y.: Doubleday Image Books, 1966), 332–33. In supporting his reference to Aquinas, Maritain cites S.T., II-II, 45, 2.

5. This caricature has been, rightly, criticized by Pope John Paul II; see "Veritatis Splendor," *Origins* 23:18 (October 14, 1993): §§65–70. A detailed discussion of the critique, and a demonstration of the fact that it responds not to an accurate understanding of fundamental option but to a caricature are presented in my article "The Question of *Grundentscheidung*," *Theology and Philosophy*, forthcoming.

6. This present author was one of the first to recommend this adjustment, in *Principles for a Catholic Morality* (New York: Seabury Press, 1978), 64. The approach was given support by Richard Gula, *Reason Informed by Faith* (New York: Paulist Press, 1989), 79f.

7. E.g., my *Principles for a Catholic Morality*, revised edition (San Francisco: Harper & Row, 1990), 74–76.

8. The idea of impediments and their significance for contemporary moral theology is developed more fully in my *Principles for a Catholic Morality*, revised edition, 53–57.

9. A wonderfully positive alternative is offered by Simon Harak, *Virtuous Passions* (New York: Paulist Press, 1993).

10. This terminology, first introduced in "The Theology of Conscience," *Chicago Studies* 14 (1976): 149–66, is developed in greater detail in *Principles for a Catholic Morality*, revised edition, 103–18.

4

The Virtuous Disciple

THE VISION OF THE HUMAN PERSON THAT HAS BEEN PRESENTED
in the last two chapters represents the best of Roman Catholic moral
theology, as that science has developed over the last several centuries.
In many ways this vision has much to commend it. In many of its details
it strikes one as being accurate, and it seems responsive to much of the
subtlety and ambiguity that is part of human experience. At the same
time, the vision is not without its flaws. It is marred at least by partiality, if not by actual error. And so there is need to complete the first part
of this book by presenting some additional perspectives recently developed by scholars in their considerations of the human person.

Specifically, what needs to be added to the traditional understanding is a much more conscious awareness of the process of human development. Human beings change and grow, and this change and growth
are critical components of the moral life. In this chapter, then, I shall
present two sets of reflections which together provide an additional
dimension to the understanding of the human person. The first set
explores the idea of virtue, while the second brings to bear recent psychological insights into the process of human development.

Vision of Human Virtue

The recent renewal of the vision of the human person in Catholic
moral theology, a renewal that significantly advances the perspectives
presented in the last two chapters, can be dated from the landmark
book *After Virtue,* by Alasdair MacIntyre.[1] This book is a broad-ranging

critique of moral philosophy in the modern and contemporary eras. MacIntyre develops his critique by confronting more recent perspectives with those presented by the ancients, from Plato and Aristotle to Thomas Aquinas. And he finds a strong contrast.

The ancient visions did not simply focus on human acts. They also gave serious attention to the context within which those acts took on significance. One way of looking at that context is to focus on the objective moral order, as we did in chapter 2. This order is such that by embracing it and conforming to it the human person achieves a true happiness. That is, the order is not merely some legalistic imposition; rather, it is an accurate description of what genuinely allows for human flourishing. But if this is true, then the objective vision can be described not only in terms of external behaviors, but also in terms of human personal styles, and this represents a second way of describing the moral context.

For example, human persons ought to tell the truth. This does not simply mean that each individual act ought to be a truthful act. It also means that the human person ought to habitually and characteristically tell the truth. So much is this so that if a human person has the consistent style and practice of truthfulness we can describe that person as good, as successful, as fulfilling the expectation of how life ought to be. To describe the human person as "truthful," or "honest," is, of course, to describe virtues that ought to characterize the human person. So, from the perspective of this ancient morality, what is good can be described either in terms of appropriate external behavior, right acts, or in terms of appropriate internal personal styles and approaches and characteristic ways of behaving, the virtues.

But, beginning with the Enlightenment, argues MacIntyre, this entire vision of an objective moral order was lost. In its place came an exalted appreciation for human freedom (that relativism which we discussed earlier), so much so that human success and human flourishing were understood to be nothing else than the thoroughgoing expression of human freedom. From that point of view, one can only describe the good person as one who does whatever she or he does in a genuinely free and uncompelled manner. One cannot describe and dictate the sorts of behaviors that should be performed or the sorts of behavioral approaches that ought to be present in the human person. Thus, MacIntyre can say that it is our sad fate to live "after virtue."

MacIntyre is convinced that this situation has caused a wide range of maladies. Our purposes in this book do not require us to analyze them in detail. What we do need to understand is that his critique has led to a broad reexploration of that vision of human virtue that was proclaimed by older writers. And to the extent that Catholic moral theology has participated in that renewal, we can see our moment as a moment in which there is a retrieval of virtue.

To understand what this retrieval entails, let us describe in a bit more detail the traditional view of virtue, particularly as it was articulated by Thomas Aquinas. As was pointed out in chapter 3, traditional Roman Catholic moral theology began its discussion of human behavior by looking at the "human act." To that extent the theological system sounds as if it focused only on behavior. But in the case of Aquinas this was not true. Aquinas did talk about the human act, but he saw that act as connected to other human acts to the point that they became characteristic of the person who is the human agent. And so, in analyzing the components of the human act, Aquinas laid particular emphasis on the reality of human *habits*.

As that term is used in modern English, it has an almost pejorative tone: "I have a bad habit of swearing." Hence, habit as an impediment, as we discussed in the last chapter. But this was not the case in Aquinas's usage. For him a habit is a human achievement, a developed skill whereby persons are able to perform human acts with both authenticity and fluidity. When we turn on the television to the golf matches of a Sunday afternoon, we are seeing people who possess to a high degree the "habit" of playing golf. That is, they have achieved such an integration of a variety of activities that they can perform them predictably, almost automatically, and with a high degree of success. In one sense, their acts are less "intentional" than the acts of those who lack this habit. That is, paradoxically, the person who has the habit does not need to think as much as one who lacks it. But the absence of this rational thought does not indicate a deficiency of the human act; rather it signifies an achievement. For the person who possesses the habit has transcended the need for rational thought, has so integrated the various components of the act that they have become "connatural."[2]

The golfers have, of course, an athletic habit. One can similarly talk of intellectual habits. The person who is able to read these pages at a high rate of speed and with a high degree of comprehension, for example, has a habit of reading that represents a very attractive human achievement. At the same time, one does not presume that either golfers or readers are genuinely good persons. These particular habits involve acts that are "good in a certain respect." For Aquinas, however, there are also some habits that involve acts that are "good understood simply." These are integrated abilities to perform acts that are good in an overall and comprehensive way. In this sense, we speak of people who have that habit of truthfulness, the habit of honor, the habit of chastity, and the like. These habits are known as virtues.

Put simply, then, virtues are integrated human skills whereby a person is able to, and tends to, perform genuinely good acts. Indeed, the person is able to, and tends to, perform these acts in a predictable and integrated fashion to such a degree that the good acts can truly be described as characteristic of the person in question. Thus, we can speak of the person as virtuous, in the same way that we speak of the acts as objectively moral.

Virtue in Moral Theology

This traditional Thomistic understanding has received broad attention in recent years, and this attention has led to a substantial retrieval of its wisdom. Among Roman Catholic authors, perhaps Jean Porter has made the most substantial contribution. In a series of publications over the last ten years she has joined careful analysis of the writings of Thomas Aquinas to the various issues and concerns of contemporary moral philosophy and moral theology. In this way she has helped to generate a contemporary understanding of the moral virtues.[3] Similarly helpful is the Dominican scholar Romanus Cessario.[4]

Ironically, however, given that we are referring to the discussion of Thomas Aquinas, perhaps the greater impetus for this renewal has come from Protestant ethicists. The initial impetus for this renewal can be located in the writings of James Gustafson, perhaps the foremost Protestant ethicist of the second half of the twentieth century. His book *Christ and the Moral Life* addresses the question of whether Christian faith makes a difference in the living of the moral life. Over a series of chapters, Gustafson discusses the various roles that Christ, and faith in Christ, has for the Christian in the living out of moral behavior. He then summarizes his conclusions in a final chapter that is a landmark.

> I propose to explore a way of interpreting and explicating Christian moral life, regarding particularly some of the differences faith in Jesus Christ *often does make, can make, and ought to make* in the moral lives of the members of the Christian community. . . . First . . . is a delineation of a perspective, a fundamental angle of vision and posture of life that

the Christian gospel enables and requires. Second is . . . the attitudes and dispositions that are evoked and shaped by loyalty to Jesus Christ. This is followed by . . . the fundamental intentions, purposes, and ends that are consummate with Christian faith. . . . Finally, . . . Christ and his teaching provide norms to be brought to bear in particular moral judgments.[5]

But what are these "postures," "attitudes," "fundamental intentions, purposes, and ends," and "norms" that Gustafson is talking about? One cannot help noticing the similarity of his language to the language of the virtues. Indeed, in discussing his second category, "dispositions," Gustafson makes the matter explicit. "Dispositions are 'habits' in the classic Roman Catholic use of that term; not mechanical automatic responses to external stimuli, but persisting tendencies to act in such a way that one's action is directed in part by these lasting dispositions."[6] And again, "the traditional language of virtue pointed toward this aspect of human experience. St. Thomas wrote that a virtue is a 'lasting disposition' that is in accord with a being's true nature and true end."[7]

Virtue and Character

But if Gustafson led the way in stimulating reconsideration of the Thomistic notion of virtues, his student and protégé Stanley Hauerwas is the person who has most dramatically advanced the discussion.

Although Hauerwas has developed his thoughts in this area in a large selection of publications, his most focused discussion is in *Character and the Christian Life: A Study in Theological Ethics*. He is candid in acknowledging that the content of this book was itself first developed in a doctoral dissertation written under the supervision of James Gustafson. The heritage for these ideas is, therefore, obvious. But what is Hauerwas's point? "The basic thesis claims that Christian ethics is best understood as an ethics of character since the Christian moral life is fundamentally an orientation of the self."[8]

So in focusing on Christian character Hauerwas is asking us to move the spotlight from exterior behavior to the style, approach, perspectives, and inclinations of the human person. This new focus is, of course, intimately related to the understanding of the virtues that goes back to Thomas Aquinas. Interestingly, however, Hauerwas does not understand character and virtue to be synonymous. He suggests that the virtues, like the idea of character, require effort on the part of the agent. The idea of character, however, not only denotes a more general orientation than the virtues, but having character is a more basic moral determination of the self. The various virtues receive their particular form through the agent's character.[9]

But at the same time, in a footnote Hauerwas also declares that

in the history of moral reflection the themes associated with character and virtue have often been mixed, and whether they can ever be ultimately separated is a real question. This means that it will be necessary in Chapter Two to take some of the points made by Aristotle and Aquinas concerning virtue to apply equally to character, since for methodological purposes I am assuming that the distinction I am making between these is meaningful.[10]

I include these extensive quotations not to draw us into arid philosophical debates but only to indicate the complexity of the matter. For, at least as the terms are used colloquially, there seems to be a different connotation for character than for virtue. And, inasmuch as our purpose will be the cultivation of a Christian way of life, we will find ourselves asking both how to develop a Christian character and how to develop appropriate moral virtues.[11]

The ultimate point of these sets of reflections is to highlight the recent shift from a single-minded focus on either exterior behavior or abiding internal identity to an appreciation for the process of human growth and development. This retrieval of the tradition of the virtues and the introduction of the term "character" so forcefully presented by Hauerwas represent a new moment in Christian moral theology, a moment that highlights the degree to which Christian life is a *project* and not a possession. And by highlighting this fact, it provides a very important basis for the questions that will occupy us through the remainder of this book. To put the matter succinctly, those who practice Christian ministry are interested in evoking within the people they serve a particular way of life known from time immemorial as "discipleship." How can ministers be more effective in stimulating both the desire for, and the tendency to, engage in that life? To the extent that the discussion of virtues invites us to consider this question, and in particular to focus on the challenge of influencing human development, to that extent it serves as the preamble to our more specific agenda.

One further point needs to be made, however, before we leave the topic of virtue. In the discussion of virtue (and character) from the

Greek philosophers to the present, there seem to be two dimensions that ought to be distinguished. The virtues are, on the one hand, an *inclination* to behave in a certain way. That is to say, they represent a honing of the *will*, a focusing of the intention, so that a person abidingly and characteristically chooses to act in a certain way to such a degree that the choosing and acting occur almost automatically. But virtues also involve an *ability* to act in a certain way. That is, to the extent that a person has prudence or fortitude or chastity, to that extent the person, not unlike the golfer, has the ability to make judgments that successfully incarnate those virtues in right behavior, selecting the behavioral option that is in fact actually prudent or truly courageous or authentically chaste. In some ways, then, the virtues involve also a honing of the *intellect*, a focusing of the attention, inasmuch as they develop a skill, an ability to choose and act in a way that truly incarnates the goal of the particular virtue.

This distinction is important for us because it helps us to further define the task that will occupy us for the remainder of this book. If ministers wish to cultivate in the people of God a virtuous lifestyle, they will need to facilitate both the reinforcing of commitment that is implied by the word "inclination" and the honing of insight and activity that is implied by "skill." In both of these senses, the minister will need to serve the process of developing virtue in the Christian person.

Views of Human Development

Recent developments, not so much on the part of theologians or philosophers as on the part of social scientists, have also contributed to establishing a basis for our exploration. The entire upcoming second part of this book will mine the social sciences for insights into the dynamics of "making disciples." We dare not preempt that investigation here. But attention to one particular set of ideas will be appropriate, since they will function as premise for, rather than component of, our project.

As mentioned at the beginning of this chapter, what has developed in recent years is a renewed appreciation for the reality of human moral development. This appreciation is exemplified by, and nurtured by, the field of developmental psychology and, as a component of that field, by models of human development. There are several such models, though they all have in common a key idea: that human beings go through particular life stages that are relatively consistent and therefore predictable. Before concluding this chapter, I want to look briefly at a few of them.

Most scholars would date this emphasis upon models of developmental stages from the writings of Jean Piaget.[12] Piaget's work was primarily with small children, and his research led him to the conclusion that they go through predictable stages in the development of their cognitive and perceptual abilities. By studying the way children in the first twelve years of life played with one another, Piaget began to discern predictable changes in the ways they engaged the rules of their games. Reflecting on these changing appreciations for rules allowed him to develop some conclusions regarding the understandings of morality that these children possessed. The following two charts indicate the nature of this evolution, as it is applied to the practice of rules and to the understanding of rules.

MORAL DEVELOPMENT

Table I. Stages in the Practice of Rules

Ages   0 1 2 3 4 5 6 7 8 9 10 11 12
Codification
Cooperation
Egocentric
Motor

Table II. Stages in Consciousness of Rules

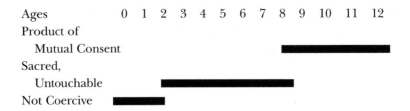

Ages   0 1 2 3 4 5 6 7 8 9 10 11 12
Product of
   Mutual Consent
Sacred,
   Untouchable
Not Coercive

Source: Reprinted, by permission of the publisher, from Ronald Duska and Mariellen Whelan, *Moral Development: A Guide to Piaget and Kohlberg* (New York: Paulist Press, 1975), 12.

A much more comprehensive view of human development was articulated by psychologist Erik Erikson.[13] Erikson is famous for his description of eight stages of human development, from birth to death. His conviction was that this developmental process is unvarying and that, if the various stages are not successfully traversed, there is the need to return and complete the processes. In other words, additional development demands that a person have negotiated earlier crises successfully. Thus, Erikson's vision of human development is, at the same time, something of a strategy for psychotherapy. The chart on p. 48 summarizes many of the insights of Erikson. Of particular interest is column B, which describes psychosocial crises. These crises concern the developmental tasks about which people often converse when they are focusing on Erikson's work. As one can see, the infancy stage involves trying to achieve trust with the world outside. Then, in order, the issues of autonomy, initiative, industry, identity, intimacy, generativity, and integrity are joined. Also worth noting are the "basic strengths" detailed in column D, especially since these have also been referred to as "virtues"![14]

It is beyond the possibilities of this book, and our needs, to go into detail about Erikson's theories. Suffice it to say that there is much to reflect on both in the overall concept of unvarying developmental stages and in the way in which he describes the developmental process of the human person.

More recently, American psychologist Daniel Levinson has proposed a typology for adult development.[15] Levinson is quite firm in asserting that he did not develop this vision from a theoretical starting point, a hypothesis he set out to prove. Rather, he claims that, somewhat to his surprise, he discovered this pattern in analyzing the experiences of a large pool of research subjects.

The chart on p. 49 summarizes Levinson's understanding. One will see that there are four "eras": early adulthood, adulthood, middle adulthood, and late adulthood. One of the interesting things about Levinson's theory is his notion that fully one third of adult life is spent in the times of transition, with only two-thirds of the time spent within firm and well-integrated stages of life. These times of transition are, as one would expect, more difficult. One's vision of life begins to unravel as it is discerned to be inadequate. There is a time of "not being sure." And only after extensive living and reflection is the person in a position to construct a new synthesis more adequate to the experience of life. Thus, Levinson's vision suggests a painful and somewhat fluid

Chart 1		A Psychosexual Stages and Modes	B Psychosocial Crises	C Radius of Significant Relations	D Basic Strengths	E Core Pathology Basic Antipathies	F Related Principles of SocialOrder	G Binding-Ritualizations	H Ritualism
	Stages								
I	Infancy	Oral-Respiratory Sensory-Kinesthetic (Incorporative Modes)	Basic Trust vs. Basic Mistrust	Maternal Person	Hope	Withdrawal	Cosmic Order	Numinous	Idolism
II	Early Childhood	Anal-Urethral, Muscular (Retentive-Eliminative)	Autonomy vs. Shame, Doubt	Parental Persons	Will	Compulsion	"Law and Order"	Judicious	Legalism
III	Play Age	Infantile-Genital Loco-motor (Intrusive, Inclusive)	Initiative vs. Guilt	Basic Family	Purpose`	Inhibition	Ideal Proto-types	Dramatic	Moralism
IV	School Age	"Latency"	Industry vs. Inferiority	"Neighbor-hood," School	Competence	Inertia	Technologi-cal Order	Formal (Technical)	Formalism
V	Adolescence	Puberty	Identity vs. Identity Con-fusion	Peer Groups and Outgroups Models of Leadership	Fidelity	Repudiation	Ideological Worldview	Ideological	Totalism
VI	Young Adulthood	Genitality	Intimacy vs. Isolation	Partners in friendship, sex, competition, cooperation	Love	Exclusivity	Patterns of Cooperation and Competi-tion	Affiliative	Elitism
VII	Adulthood	(Procreativity)	Generativity vs. Stagnation	Divided Labor and shared household	Care	Rejectivity	Currents of Education and Tradition	Generational	Authoritism
VIII	Old Age	(Generalization of Sensual Modes)	Integrity vs. Despair	"Mankind" "My Kind"	Wisdom	Disdain	Wisdom	Philosophical	Dogmatism

Source: Reprinted, with permission of the publisher, from Erik K. Erikson, *The Life Cycle Completed* (New York: Norton & Co., 1982, 32–33).

Figure 1
Developmental Periods in the Eras of Early and Middle Adulthood

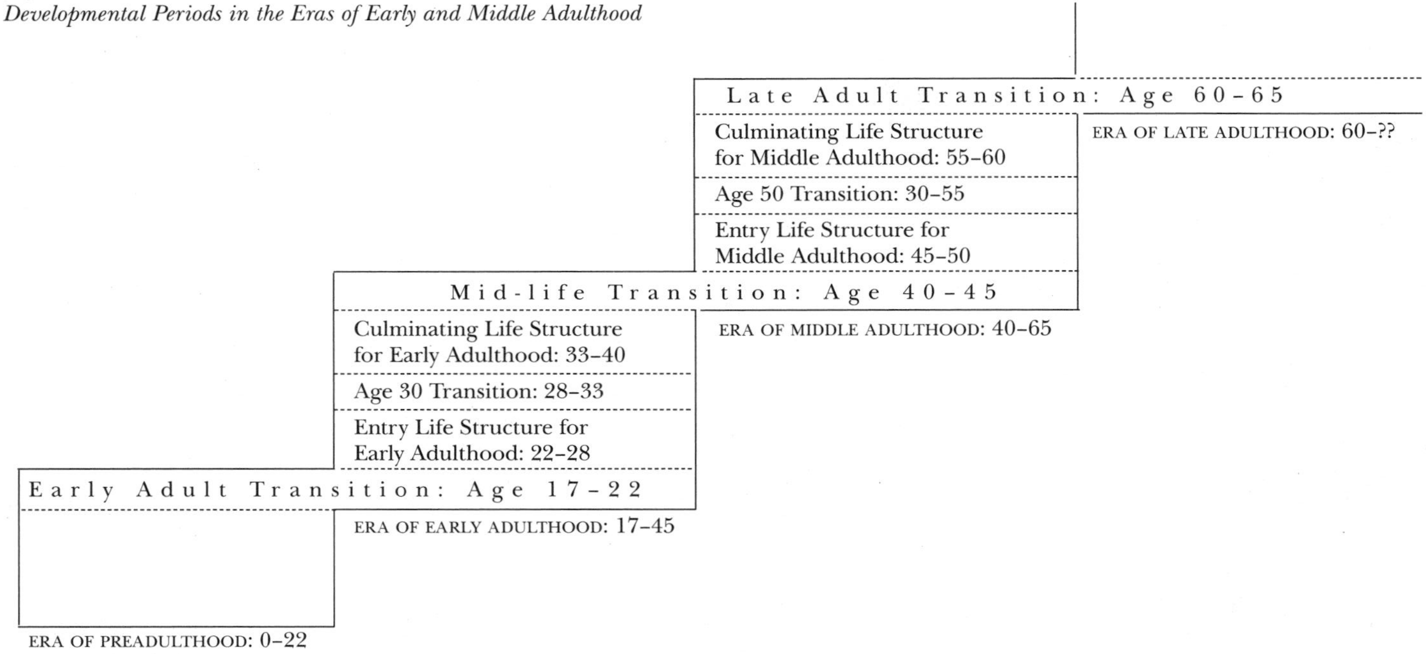

Late Adult Transition: Age 60-65

ERA OF LATE ADULTHOOD: 60-??

Culminating Life Structure
for Middle Adulthood: 55-60

Age 50 Transition: 30-55

Entry Life Structure for
Middle Adulthood: 45-50

Mid-life Transition: Age 40-45

ERA OF MIDDLE ADULTHOOD: 40-65

Culminating Life Structure
for Early Adulthood: 33-40

Age 30 Transition: 28-33

Entry Life Structure for
Early Adulthood: 22-28

Early Adult Transition: Age 17-22

ERA OF EARLY ADULTHOOD: 17-45

ERA OF PREADULTHOOD: 0-22

Note. This is an expanded adaptation of an earlier version that appeared in *The Seasons of a Man's Life* (p. 57) by D. J. Levinson et al., 1978, New York: Alfred A. Knopf, Inc. Copyright 1978 by Alfred A. Knopf, Inc. Adapted by permission.

Source: Reprinted, with permission of the publisher, from Daniel J. Levinson, "A Conception of Adult Development," *American Psychologist* 41 (January 1986): 8.

process in which people move from vision to confusion to vision over
the course of their adult years.

Faith Development

These three models of human development have in common that they
are the creations of psychologists who are focusing on the broad range
of human functioning. Their visions are not explicitly intended to
serve the needs of religion or of ethics. But there are authors who have
addressed religious questions in a way that tries to blend social science
research in the field of developmental psychology with religious concerns.[16] James Fowler is famous for his attempt to articulate stages in
the development of faith. Fowler's conviction is that, as persons go
through stages of human development, their relationship to the tran-
scendent similarly evolves. Consequently, if one is going to nurture the
faith of persons, one must be aware of the stage of the person's life, the
way in which faith functions in that life, and the sorts of needs it meets
and challenges it presents.

Fowler's model is strongly dependent on the work of Erik Erikson
and, to a lesser extent, of Daniel Levinson. The chart on the next page
indicates some parallels between the visions of these authors. One will
see that Fowler postulates six faith stages, from intuitive-projective
through universalizing. His models suggest that the development of a
truly mature and integrated faith is a lifelong project, only slowly
achieved by the human person.

Finally, we turn to the work of Lawrence Kohlberg. When one discusses social science work in developmental psychology as that work
has impacted understandings of the moral life, no one is more commonly discussed than Kohlberg.[17] His research is extensive, though not
without controversy.[18] Kohlberg's vision is that there are stages of
moral development through which human persons proceed in a predictable fashion. These stages are, for Kohlberg, characterized by ways
of *knowing* what is moral and what is not. That is, they are developmental stages in moral understanding.

One moves through these stages in response to the rather unpleasant experience of "cognitive dissonance." This is the experience where
one's current understanding proves inadequate to one's experience
and one's moral intuitions. Kohlberg's research, therefore, involved
presenting people with moral dilemmas and observing how they
thought through the dilemmas. The reason for using dilemmas was so
that particular ways of understanding could not too easily generate an

Levinson's Eras and Erikson's Psychosocial Stages	*Fowler's Faith Stages*
Era of Infancy, Childhood and Adolescence	
Trust vs. Mistrust	Undifferentiated Faith (Infancy)
Autonomy vs. Shame & Doubt	1. Intuitive Projective Faith
Initiative vs. Guilt	(Early Childhood)
Industry vs. Inferiority	2. Mythic-Literal Faith (School Years)
Identity vs. Role Confusion	3. Synthetic Conventional Faith (Adolescence)
First Adult Era	
Intimacy vs. Isolation	4. Individuative-Reflective Faith (Young Adulthood)
Middle Adult Era	
Generativity vs. Stagnation	5. Conjunctive Faith (Mid-life and beyond)
Late Adult Era	
Integrity vs. Despair	6. Universalizing Faith

From *Stages of Faith* by James W. Fowler © by James Fowler, 1981.

Source: Reprinted, with permission of the publisher, from *Faith Development in the Adult Life Cycle,* ed. Kenneth Stokes (New York: Sadlier, 1982), 195.

answer. Kohlberg's six stages (sometimes understood as three stages, each with two subdivisions) move from the sense that things are right simply because they are permitted and approved by the person in power to the sense that things are right because they are consistent with universal principles.

The stages in Kohlberg's theory can be summarized as follows:

Level A: Preconventional Level

Stage 1: The Stage of Punishment and Obedience. Right is literal obedience to rules and authority, avoiding punishment, and not doing physical harm. This stage takes an egocentric point of view.

Stage 2: The Stage of Individual Instrumental Purpose and Exchange. Right is serving one's own or others' needs and making fair deals in terms of concrete exchange. This stage takes a concrete individualistic perspective.

Level B: Conventional Level

Stage 3:   The Stage of Mutual Interpersonal Expectations, Relationships, and Conformity. Right is playing a good (nice) role, being concerned about other people and their feelings, keeping loyalty and trust with partners, and being motivated to follow rules and expectations. This stage takes the perspective of the individual in relationship to other individuals.

Stage 4:   The Stage of Social System and Conscience Maintenance. Right is doing one's duty in society, upholding the social order, and maintaining the welfare of society or the group. This stage differentiates societal point of view from interpersonal agreement or motives.

Level C: Postconventional and Principled Level

Stage 5:   The Stage of Prior Rights and Social Contract or Utility. Right is upholding the basic rights, values, and legal contracts of a society, even when they conflict with the concrete rules and laws of the group. This stage takes a prior-to-society perspective—that of a rational individual aware of values and rights prior to social attachments and contracts.

Stage 6:   The Stage of Universal, Ethical Principles. The stage assumes guidance by universal, ethical principles that all humanity should follow. This stage takes the perspective of a moral point of view from which social arrangements derive, or on which they are grounded. The perspective is that of any rational individual recognizing the nature of morality or the basic premise of respect for other persons as ends, not means.[19]

As in the other understandings that we have considered, the research of Kohlberg offers many fascinating insights. But it has been critiqued from several points of view. Carol Gilligan, for one, has pointed out that Kohlberg's research seems to presume a characteristically masculine way of thinking and understanding.[20] She suggests that women do not achieve full maturity through an understanding of morality that focuses on universal principles. Rather, her research indicates that women understand morality as rooted in relational realities. Thus, full maturity has much to do with properly integrating oneself with others and not only with the autonomous self, a perspective that for Kohlberg might seem somehow immature.

Conclusion

Craig Dykstra has more radically critiqued the work of Kohlberg,[21] and his comments will ably serve us as we bring this survey to a close. Dykstra suggests that, by focusing on how people intellectualize about moral judgments, Kohlberg has avoided a more central question. That question involves how people embrace particular values as genuinely important to them. That is, in the long haul it may be less important how people think about morality and more important whether they are committed to living the moral life.

Dykstra's question is our question too. It makes little sense for moral theology to provide detailed outlines of how one ought to live or of the dynamics of good human choice, if people do not choose to live that way. Sooner or later the minister must ask the question: How can I help develop Christian character in my people? How can I cultivate the virtues, both as skills and as inclinations, within them? How can I support the process of moral maturation so that it will issue in genuine commitment? How, indeed, can I be more successful in inviting my people into the life of intentional discipleship? How can I, in the treasured biblical phrase, make disciples unto the Lord?

The remainder of this book will attempt to answer these questions.

Notes

1. Alasdair MacIntyre, *After Virtue* (Notre Dame, Ind.: University of Notre Dame Press, 1981).

2. The term is associated with Jacques Maritain; see, e.g., *A Maritain Reader* (Garden City, N.Y.: Image Books, 1966), 332–34.

3. See especially Jean Porter, *Recovery of Virtue: The Relevance of Aquinas for Christian Ethics* (Louisville, Ky.: Westminster/John Knox Press, 1990); and "The Unity of the Virtues and the Ambiguity of Goodness: A Reappraisal of Aquinas' Theory of the Virtues," *Journal of Religious Ethics* 21 (1993): 137–64. An excellent, concise presentation of Aquinas's understanding of virtues can be found in her *Moral Action and Christian Ethics* (Cambridge: Cambridge University Press, 1995), 138–43.

4. Romanus Cessario, *The Moral Virtues and Theological Ethics* (Notre Dame, Ind.: University of Notre Dame Press, 1991). Note especially his explanation of the connection between the ideas of virtue and *habitus* (pp. 34–44).

5. James Gustafson, *Christ and the Moral Life* (Notre Dame, Ind.: University of Notre Dame Press, 1968), 240.

6. Ibid., 248.

7. Ibid., 249.

8. Stanley Hauerwas, *Character and the Christian Life: A Study in Theological Ethics* (San Antonio, Tex.: Trinity University Press, 1975), vii.

9. Ibid., 16.

10. Ibid.

11. Romanus Cessario seems to identify virtue and character in his study cited above, and Jean Porter, in her *Moral Action and Christian Ethics*, apparently in contrast to Gustafson, seems to identify virtues with dispositions: "Thus, virtue, which enables the human person to act well, that is to say, in accordance with her specific nature as a rational animal, can be understood as a disposition by which the human soul is informed by reason" (p. 140).

12. See, e.g., Jean Piaget, *The Moral Judgment of the Child* (New York: Free Press, 1965).

13. A recent concise summary of his theory can be found in Judith Caron, *Christian Ethics* (Mystic, Conn.: Twenty-Third Publications, 1995), 12–16; see also John W. Crossin, *What Are They Saying About Virtue?* (New York: Paulist Press, 1985), 58–69.

14. Crossin, *What Are They Saying*, 70, quoting Erikson to this effect also.

15. Daniel Levinson, "A Conception of Adult Development," *American Psychologist* 41 (January 1986): 3–13.

16. A general overview of these approaches, as well as the more strictly psychological theories we have just reviewed, is in *Faith Development in the Adult Life Cycle*, ed. Kenneth Stokes (New York: W. H. Sadlier, 1982).

17. For a concise summary of Kohlberg's theory, see Crossin, *What Are They Saying*, 82–86. A more comprehensive presentation is in *Moral Development: A Guide to Piaget and Kohlberg*, ed. Ronald Duska and Mariellen Whelan (New York: Paulist Press, 1975), 42–79. Kohlberg's influence is evident from *Moral Development, Moral Education, and Kohlberg*, ed. Brenda Munsey (Birmingham, Ala.: Religious Education Press, 1980).

18. See, e.g., Charles M. Shelton, *Morality of the Heart* (New York: Crossroad, 1990), 15–32. Crossin also includes critical comments (*What Are They Saying*, 87–91). And the Munsey volume cited above comprises evaluative comments, both positive and negative, along with a response by Kohlberg himself.

19. Crossin, *What Are They Saying*, 83–84. Crossin in turn cites Lawrence Kohlberg, *Essays on Moral Development*, vol. 1, *The Philosophy of Moral Development* (San Francisco: Harper & Row, 1981), 409–12.

20. Carol Gilligan, *In A Different Voice: Psychological Theory and Women's Development* (Cambridge: Harvard University Press, 1982).

21. Craig Dykstra, *Vision and Character* (New York: Paulist Press, 1981), 7–29.

PART 2

INSIGHTS FROM THE

SOCIAL SCIENCES

5

The Values People Live

IN OUR DISCUSSION OF THE CATHOLIC MORAL TRADITION, WE HAVE found that the notion of "value" plays a central role. We have also found that the term has a very specific meaning. In chapter 2 we saw that values are realities or aspects of reality that are important in themselves, that command our respect and observance, and that call for a response in our everyday behavior.

Now, in this second part of our investigation, we will be talking about "values" again. But the word will have a quite different meaning, and it is absolutely essential to be aware of the shift of meaning that is taking place. From now on, "value" refers to realities or aspects of reality that are in fact esteemed by particular persons. That is, we are talking about what people *really* value, what they appreciate. If we define the first use of the term, the theological use, as "objective" values, we can describe the second use as "subjective" values. But this is not a pejorative term, as if we were to say they are "merely" subjective values. Rather, it is a neutral term, simply acknowledging that our focus is on what actual individual subjects truly value.

The two meanings of our term, and their relationship to each other, can be made clear by considering the following sentence: Mature persons acknowledge that classical music is a value, but many adults—and almost all teenagers—do not value it. As the sentence makes clear, there is a very substantial difference between "value" as what is important in itself and "value" as what a person cherishes. But the difference is not only substantial; it is also significant. Indeed, the sentence not only exemplifies the shift of terminology that we are identifying. It also defines the project on which we are now embarking. Put simply, the central question of this book is: how can we encourage people to *value* Christian *values?* How can we turn [objective] values into [subjective] values?

In one sense we have already embarked on this project. In chapter 4 we defined "virtues" as both *abilities* and *inclinations* to do the good. In so doing, we acknowledged that just because honesty, for example, is judged by the Christian tradition to be a value, it does not follow that persons who call themselves Christian value it. They may not be *inclined* toward the behavior that we claim is valuable. And if that is the case, then it is not really a value for them.

So, in one sense the call for the development of virtues is nothing other than a call for the rendering into subjective values of the objective values of the tradition. Following this line, we can say that our project for the remainder of this book will be the development of virtue or, alternatively, the development of strategies that will increase the likelihood that (objective) values will also be (subjective) values.

The Study of Values

In pursuing this project, we will turn to a wide range of research in the social sciences. For, as we shall see, psychologists and sociologists have given a great deal of attention to the reality of [subjective] values. And through their research they have come to considerable insight on the questions of where a person's values come from, how they are influenced, and by what means they can be modified.

We can begin our turn to the social sciences through a brief look at the work of psychologist Milton Rokeach, whose work will help us become even clearer about this precise distinction between (objective) and (subjective) values. It will also enrich these ideas and help us focus our project. At the same time, as we shall see, it will also allow us to ease our turn to the social sciences by making some important connections to the theological ideas we have already pursued.

From the mid 1960s, and until his death in 1988, Milton Rokeach pursued a project of ongoing research intended to identify what Americans truly value. How did he do this? First, Rokeach establishes a definition: "A value is an enduring belief that a specific mode of conduct or end-state of existence is personally or socially preferable to an opposite or converse mode of conduct or end-state of existence."[1] As one would expect, the various elements of the definition are important. Let's expand on them.

Rokeach says that a value is a belief. To my mind the term "belief" sounds rather intellectual; indeed, some authors seem to contrast beliefs and values, stating that beliefs are convictions one proclaims whereas values are convictions actually lived out. Rokeach, however, is not using the term in this intellectual way. For him, "values, like all beliefs, have cognitive, affective, and behavioral components."[2] So they are fully integrated aspects of a person.

Then Rokeach says that values involve a "specific mode of conduct or end-state of existence." These two are not synonyms; they are alternatives. For Rokeach, some values describe how we would like things to be (end-states of existence). These he calls "terminal values." Other values describe ways of living that we believe will get us to that end-state (modes of conduct). These he calls "instrumental values."

Third, Rokeach declares that one holds particular values because they are viewed as either "personally or socially preferable." Again, these two represent alternatives. Some people seem to embrace values because they are perceived as desirable for the self; in other cases the focus seems to be on values that are desirable for the community. In the case of terminal values, Rokeach describes these two as "personal" and "social" respectively. In the case of instrumental values, he names self-oriented values as "competence" and community-oriented ones as "moral." These last terms may seem more than just nomenclature; they may seem to involve a position Rokeach is intentionally taking: that is, that some people are "selfish" and others are "moral." But that does not seem to be the intent of his jargon. Really, he is simply saying that, when it comes to modes of behavior that people cherish, some people seem to emphasize those modes that are expressions of self-actualization, others those that are expressions of mutual responsibility. And of that fact there can hardly be question.

Values as Preferences

The last element of the definition to be isolated is Rokeach's description of values as "preferences." But this element requires much more consideration on our part, for it carries within it an assertion that is central to Rokeach's work. So let us turn to this second element of Rokeach's vision: his assertion that (subjective) values are not affirmations but preferences.

What does he mean? Essentially, Rokeach is arguing that when people talk about values, they tend to spend many words distinguishing between good and bad, between values and disvalues. But that's a useless task, since it belabors the obvious. No one is going to claim, for example, that laziness is a value, although many people are evidently lazy. Similarly, no one is likely to hold that trustworthiness is bad, although many people evidently fail to live in this way. Thus, precisely because of the cultural force that value terms such as "lazy" or "trustworthy" have, they are preset to be either bad or good. And the person being queried about values knows implicitly what ought to be said in affirming the good and rejecting the bad.

The issue, then, in Rokeach's mind, is not affirmation but rather preference. In a situation of conflict, which (admittedly good value) is given priority? For example, people are not likely to say that Beethoven's music is bad, or even unimportant. But some people are very likely to select a CD not of Beethoven but of the rock group of the moment for playing on their home stereo. And they may do this consistently! It is not that they have particular animus against Beethoven; it's just that they *prefer* the rock group. So, if we want to understand rightly the values out of which people actually live, it is less important to discuss "intrinsic worth" than it is to consider "relative preference."

This premise of Rokeach's is very helpful to us. If we say that followers of Jesus ought to prefer fidelity to comfort, that they ought to keep their promises even at personal inconvenience, we are not saying that comfort is a bad thing. We are simply saying that, in our judgment, it is not as important a value as fidelity to promises. Thus, if we succeed in the project of moral formation, our success will be manifested not precisely by the fact that people despise comfort, but rather by the fact that they hold and enact this preference for fidelity. Similarly, persons who fail to keep their promises because it is inconvenient to do so are probably not saying that promise keeping is a positive *disvalue*. They are simply saying that it is not as important to them as convenience.

If this is true, then the project of moral formation, the making of disciples, is a project not of "value-affirmation creation" but of "value-preference modification"! This conclusion is pregnant with meaning for us. It is also intriguingly reminiscent of some of the ideas we saw in our exposition of Catholic moral theology. Recall our claim in chapter 2 that, in a finite world, all values are in competition with one another. For in such a world one cannot do all things. Rather, everything "costs"; to do one thing is to leave another undone. Consequently, all moral choices are choices among goods (i.e., [objective] values). But if this is true, then all concrete moral choices are the enactment of *preferences.* So the assertion that Rokeach offers with regard to (subjective) values resonates with the insight we have already discerned in our consideration of (objective) values.

Specific Values

Now, Rokeach builds on these two elements, his definition and his assertion, by developing a list of specific values, both terminal and instrumental, which he then proceeds to use in empirical studies. In his book *The Nature of Human Values,* Rokeach explains in great detail how he came to select the particular values he utilized in his investigation. Briefly, starting with terminal values, he and his colleagues intuitively suspected that a relatively small number of alternative futures would constitute a selection that would include the actual preferred future of most people. At one point, building on lists created by others, they developed a set of twelve terminal values. Feedback from people who felt that a value very important to them was absent led to the expansion of the set to eighteen values. These they began to utilize in research projects. Subsequent use has confirmed that most people do indeed find their own convictions about desirable end-states to be named adequately by one or another term in this relatively small list.

When it came to instrumental values, a much larger selection of alternatives seemed called for. Indeed, in his book Rokeach refers to research that has identified hundreds of "trait words" that would seem to describe these values. For purposes of his research, however, Rokeach felt a need to limit the list to a number that could be given consideration by interviewees. By a process of combination and clarification, then, the number was repeatedly reduced. In the end, for merely aesthetic reasons, a set of eighteen instrumental values—a number equal to the number of terminal values—was selected. Once again, usage has confirmed that the list provides most people with the choices they need to describe their actual preferences with reasonable accuracy. The chart on the next page provides a summary of the two lists that resulted.[3]

The next step in Rokeach's research was to administer a "Value Survey" to various populations. In each case, the list of the values, in alphabetical order as they appear in this chart, was given to the respondents. They were then asked to reorder the values, placing them in the order

Terminal Values

A comfortable life
(a prosperous life)

Family security
(taking care of loved ones)

Pleasure
(an enjoyable, leisurely life)

An exciting life
(a stimulating, active life)

Freedom
(independence, free choice)

Salvation
(saved, eternal life)

A sense of accomplishment
(lasting contribution)

Happiness
(contentedness)

Self-respect
(self-esteem)

A world at peace
(free of war and conflict)

Inner harmony
(freedom from inner conflict)

Social recognition
(respect, admiration)

A world of beauty
(beauty of nature and the arts)

Mature love
(sexual and spiritual intimacy)

True friendship
(close companionship)

Equality
(brotherhood, equal opportunity for all)

National security
(protection from attack)

Wisdom
(a mature understanding of life)

Instrumental Values

Ambitious
(hardworking, aspiring)

Forgiving
(willing to pardon others)

Logical
(consistent, rational)

Broadminded
(open-minded)

Helpful
(working for the welfare of others)

Loving
(affectionate, tender)

Capable
(competent, effective)

Honest
(sincere, truthful)

Obedient
(dutiful, respectful)

Cheerful
(lighthearted, joyful)

Imaginative
(daring, creative)

Polite
(courteous, well-mannered)

Clean
(neat, tidy)

Independent
(self-reliant, self-sufficient)

Responsible
(dependable, reliable)

Courageous
(standing up for your beliefs)

Intellectual
(intelligent, reflective)

Self-controlled
(restrained, self-disciplined)

of priority that they hold in that person's life. Sometimes the participants did this by numbering the items. In later versions they were given gummed labels that could be moved around so that the rank ordering could be visually assessed and repeatedly revised until the participant was satisfied that the ranking accurately represented her or his own priorities.

On the basis of the information gathered in this way, Rokeach developed a wide range of interpretative analyses. Different racial, ethnic, and religious groups were compared. Broad populations were compared over a period of years. And, in a few cases, specific populations were compared, before and after activities intended to encourage change in value preferences.[4]

The Insight

Since much of this research is now dated, I will not tarry over the details. Other authors will offer us more insight, when we come to consider specific methods for preference modification. For now, it is sufficient to hold clear the central insight that comes out of Rokeach's work, an insight that continues to energize psychological research and that deserves much greater attention from theologians and pastors. And what is that insight? It is this: value inculcation, the making of disciples, misunderstands its mission if it views itself as the process of convincing people that what seems good is bad, and vice versa. Rather its mission is convincing people that what seems more important is less important, and that something else is more important.

This is an important difference. Let me exemplify. I am astonished how often I hear preachers who, in the process of seeking to discourage abortion, attempt to argue that there is no such thing as a genuine conflict in this area. But there is, and the refusal to acknowledge it simply renders the preacher incredible. A pregnancy when the parents are already financially strapped is a problem. So is a pregnancy where the unborn child is known to be seriously malformed. Indeed, even an "inconvenient" pregnancy is a problem. For as real as the value of continued life may be, financial security, health, and predictability are values too. So to deny these other values, and thus the reality of the value conflicts, is to deny reality.

What is more, it is also unnecessary. To argue that a behavioral choice is wrong does not require that one prove it to be totally, unremittingly evil. No, to make the argument of wrongness, it is sufficient to argue that the choice is, on balance, unjustifiably destructive. Thus, the preacher would be both more correct and more effective if he or she would take a minute to acknowledge the reality of the other values and of the consequent value conflicts. Having done so, having acknowledged the cost involved, the preacher would still be able to assert what a person ought to do. And the preacher would be much more likely to be heard.

Examples such as this could be multiplied. When parents try to recommend sexual abstinence to their children while pretending that there is no cost or that the forgone pleasure and intimacy are not themselves true values, they simply make their argument look foolish. When students pursuing higher education are urged to eschew cheating on examinations while ignoring the conflicts, even conflicts among "higher goods," the speaker does so at the cost of credibility. When professional people are called to a lifestyle of fairness, equity, and responsibility while pretending that such behavior fits neatly and productively into our complex, contradictory world, the prophet who issues this call simply looks naive or, worse, duplicitous.

And when those who invite their sisters and brothers into a life of discipleship fail to name the "cost of discipleship," as Dietrich Bonhoeffer called it, when they fail to admit the seriousness of the reordering of value priorities they are proposing and the genuineness of the other values that the follower of Christ is asked to view as of less importance, they fail to speak the truth and honor the choices that are being sought.

For it is the reordering of preferences that is the goal of the process of moral education and formation. Any other conception is not only wrongheaded. It is also doomed to failure.

Notes

1. Milton Rokeach, *The Nature of Human Values* (New York: Free Press, 1973), 5.

2. Ibid., 7.

3. Developed from Rokeach's list (ibid., 28).

4. An interesting discussion of this research is found in Milton Rokeach, "Stability and Change in American Value Priorities: 1968–1981," *American Psychologist* 44 (1989): 775–84. Also see the response: Schuman, Steeh and Bobo, "A Clarification," *American Psychologist* 45 (1990): 674–75.

6

The Place of Feeling

THE STORY IS TOLD—AND IT IS A TRUE STORY—OF ONE PHINEAS P. GAGE, a foreman working on a crew that was building a new railroad line across Vermont in 1898. It is the story of a frightful on-the-job accident that befell him. It is also the story of a scientific discovery with fascinating implications for the topic of moral development.

The railroad right-of-way on which the crew was working passed through rugged, mountainous terrain. In Gage's role as foreman, one of his responsibilities was arranging the dynamite used to cut a path for the track. One of the crew would drill a hole in the stone. Dynamite would be placed in that hole. A fuse would be added to the dynamite. And finally, a quantity of sand would be poured in, on top of the other ingredients. Then Gage, having confirmed that all the ingredients were in the hole, would carefully tamp down the sand, using a cast iron rod about three feet long.

On this summer day, for some unexplained reason the sand had not been poured into the hole in the rock. And thus, when Gage began to tamp down the mixture, a spark set off a premature explosion. The rod shot out of the hole, flying upward. It pierced Gage's left cheek and emerged through the top of his skull, landing some distance away.

A frightful accident. Even more amazing is the fact that Gage never lost consciousness, did not experience great pain, and recovered from his injury rather quickly. All seemed to be fine. Gage could speak, think, and perform the physical functions of daily life. Everything appeared to be as before. But not so. Over the years that followed a pattern slowly emerged: Phineas Gage could do everything except organize his life. He moved from job to job, losing a succession of positions through irresponsible behavior. He became a drifter, and ultimately he died penniless in California.

Neurologist Antonio Damasio tells the story of Phineas Gage at the beginning of his amazing book *Descartes' Error.*[1] And the conclusions that Damasio reaches have broad implications for our project in understanding the appropriation of moral values.

A blessing for medical science is the fact that, after his death, the skull of Phineas Gage was recovered. Eventually it came to be housed at the medical school at Harvard University. Recently, using computer technology only available in the twentieth century, scholars have taken precise measurements of that skull and, projecting them into a three dimensional perspective, have determined the exact portions of Gage's brain that would have been disturbed by the passage of the iron rod. Armed with this information, Antonio Damasio has gone searching for contemporary individuals who had suffered brain tumors in exactly that same area, individuals whose tumors had been removed by a surgery that might have had similar effects on their brains.

Finding several individuals who fit this pattern, Damasio began to study the behavior of these individuals. The astonishing conclusion: for them as for Gage, the violation destroyed nothing of their physical or mental functions. But it did, in some strange way, undermine their ability to organize life. But what, exactly, did these individuals lack, which prevented them from taking responsibility for their lives? In the case of these contemporary individuals, Damasio was able to explore that question by giving these individuals extensive batteries of tests.

Presuming that life decisions have much to do with reasoning, Damasio at first focused on processes of reasoning. But much to his surprise, tests revealed that these processes remained intact. Intelligence was unaffected, logical processing was unaffected, verbal and motor skills were unaffected by this damage to the brain. Indeed, even when these individuals were given tests designed to assess their ability to make good judgments—for example, the moral dilemmas developed by psychologist Lawrence Kohlberg—they performed quite normally. So, in the abstract, they were perfectly capable of thinking about moral dilemmas and reasoning about choices that should be made. But they could not, in fact, make good decisions in their own lives. How come? In the end, almost by accident, one difference began to manifest itself: a lack of emotional engagement. When confronted by real choices to be enacted in their real lives, they felt neither elation nor terror. They experienced neither anxiety nor depression. Indeed, in the words of the song in the musical *A Chorus Line*, they "felt nothing."

Without recounting all the details of Damasio's research, I can summarize his conclusions. They revolve around the notion that emotion is central to human decision making. According to Damasio, René Descartes developed a perspective on the human person that suggested that reason should be as dissociated from body and feeling as possible. The ideal was that human decision making should be cool and rational. This, in Damasio's view, was "Descartes' error." In contrast to this perspective, Damasio asserts that human decision making is filled with bodily and emotional content. And, indeed, in the absence of these emotional markers, felt in the body, good decision making is not even possible.

Damasio's Conclusions

All of this can be made clearer and richer if we summarize Damasio's conclusions in a series of statements. These will include four basic facts, an overarching understanding, and a possible explanation.

The first basic fact is that the brain has differentiated parts. That is, not everything happens everywhere. This does not mean that any individual part of the brain does only one activity. On the contrary, most parts have several functions. But it does mean that we can correlate various activities with various areas of the brain. The second fact is that, in the ordinary course of things, the brain interacts with the rest of the body in two different ways (and not in one way, as is often thought). The brain "communicates" both through electrical impulses and through chemicals, such as adrenaline, which stimulates heart rate, respiration, and the like. What is more, both of these "highways of communication," the electrical and the chemical, go in both directions. That is, electrical impulses travel to the brain, as, for example, when someone stubs their toe; and the impulses travel in the opposite direction as well, as when we reach out and shake someone's hand. Similarly, chemicals are emitted both by the brain and by cells throughout the body, providing communication in both directions as they are carried through the body in the bloodstream.

Third, the brain is organized, first and foremost, to facilitate the individual's survival. That is, no matter how many activities the brain may initiate, nothing is more important than staying alive. Therefore, there is a sort of hierarchical structure to brain activities. The bottom-most level is that of the reflexes. So, for example, when the hand is touched by fire, it pulls away immediately. Here there is no need for communication between the hand and the brain. The brain has, as it were, "delegated" authority for this response to the local area so that an electrochemical reaction occurring right within the hand, responding to the pain, causes an immediate response in the form of a pulling back of that hand. The next level is one of "simple emotions." Thus, for example, many people, when they see a snake, have an almost immediate response of fear. Somehow the visual cue of the snake reaches the brain and leads to an immediate chemical response, an emission of chemicals such as adrenaline, generating a set of physical symptoms that can be called fear or anxiety. These feelings, in turn, encourage the person to flee. Finally, the same process occurs in a more sophisticated way through what Damasio calls "secondary emotions," that is, emotions developed as a result of particular experiences. Thus, a person who has survived an automobile accident may have similar emotional reactions in the presence of later similar situations.

This last comment leads to the fourth basic fact: that knowledge is stored within the memory in the form of images. First come the experiences that comprise all of our lives. Associated with these experiences are feelings, including the biochemical components of feelings that we have discussed. Then the experiences are remembered, stored in the brain as images that match the initial experiences. At later moments the memory "reappears" in the brain, an image of tremendous clarity. And when it does, the image generates the same electrochemical reactions as did the initial experience. Thus the feelings are felt once again. Damasio refers to these images as "dispositional representations." That is, they are representations that tend to "dispose" us to experience once again the particular feelings that were associated with previous experiences.

These are the four basic facts detailed by Damasio. In support of each he provides extensive neurological evidence that need not detain us. But the facts are important, and Damasio proceeds to unveil their significance by presenting an overarching understanding. The facts, he says, are true of all animals; their truth is biological. But they are also true of humans, for humans differ from other animals not by being "distinctly other" but by being "tremendously more." That is, the difference is one of extension, not of discontinuity.

Still, the extension is very important. With regard to their experiences humans have greatly developed the ability to pay attention and to remember, on the one hand, and to describe in language, on the other. Consequently, human beings have also greatly developed both the quantity and the sophistication of their dispositional representations. They have a much greater ability to evoke those dispositional representations and therefore to have the secondary emotions related to them. To take a simple example, I can refer in conversation to my grandfather's death. This may remind you of your grandfather's death. This may stimulate in you the image, the dispositional representation, of that experience, which, in turn, will stimulate a complex set of electrochemically precipitated feelings within you. This combination of attention, memory, imagination, and language is the core of that human development which goes beyond that of the other animals of our experience.

This latter set of internal events seems to be what Phineas Gage lacked. That is, he had intellectual memory, he had language. But he seems not to have had feeling. Somehow his memories did not stimulate the electrochemical emissions that led to affective response. And for some reason this absence of affect inhibited his ability to organize his life. How can this be?

Damasio's Hypothesis

This question leads to Antonio Damasio's "somatic marker hypothesis," his possible explanation. According to Damasio, we can describe Descartes' error as being a "high reason hypothesis." Descartes' position was that the organization of human life takes place through clear thinking, since the human being is most fundamentally a thinking being (*cogito, ergo sum*). In contrast to Descartes, Damasio suggests that personal decisions are profoundly emotional and bodily experiences, since the human being is an integrated, ultimately interwoven, somatic and emotional and intellectual being.

This perhaps is how it works. When I am confronted with a tough personal decision, I very quickly begin to cycle through my mind images of possible activities. Each of the images in turn stimulates particular electrochemical responses. These, in turn, stimulate feelings within my body, feelings that render the alternatives either attractive or repulsive. Since the human body is designed, first and foremost, for survival, the process of generating these feelings is quicker even than the process of thinking. Thus, in little more than a split second, a wide range of alternatives are experienced. Most of them are rejected. A few, all of which generate fundamentally positive physical feelings, remain for more intellectual consideration. Thus, building on (and depending on) this electrochemical sorting process, a final, finishing act of thinking leads to a personal judgment.

It was this absence of emotional cues, of somatic markers, that, in Damasio's opinion, made it impossible for Phineas Gage and the contemporary subjects whose brains were similarly affected to make the concrete judgments necessary for the practical organization of their lives.

Damasio provides extensive additional argumentation for this hypothesis, as the chapters of his book unfold. It is not necessary for us to review all of that. Rather, let us accept, at least as plausible, his hypothesis, and let us imagine the implications it might have for the transmission of Christian values. Put very simply, the implication is this: if Antonio Damasio's research is correct, the cultivation of values and the making of personal and moral judgments are centrally bodily and emotional processes, not just intellectual ones.

Theological Themes

At first blush, Damasio's hypothesis may seem a radical one, but it is not as unconventional as it might seem. Let us take a moment to note several formulations of theologians and philosophers that seem to be pointed in the same direction.

As we saw in chapter 3, traditional Roman Catholic moral theology has long claimed that truly human behavior requires both knowledge and freedom. And first and foremost, we cannot be responsible for what we do not know. But what sort of knowledge is involved in genuinely human action? Those of us infected with Descartes' error might be inclined to respond: clear and distinct ideas. But that was not the tradition's response. As we already saw in chapter 3, it was quite customary in the tradition to make a distinction between *cognitio speculativa* and *cognitio aestimativa*, speculative knowledge and evaluative knowledge, and to view the latter as the essential prerequisite for moral choice. Evaluative knowledge, you will recall, is knowledge that includes a personally felt appreciation for the significance of the information known.

So the tradition seems to have valued feeling more than might be suspected. Indeed, the degree to which the theological tradition supported this "Damasio-esque" perspective will be revealed through an interesting example. In 1968 Pope Paul VI issued the encyclical *Humanae Vitae,* including its famous condemnation of artificial contraception. A subsequent question quickly arose: What shall we make of the many Catholics who seem not to understand this condemnation as compelling for themselves? In an article in *Chicago Studies,* theologian John Dedek offered a fascinating response. Dedek pointed out that it was obvious, given the widespread media attention, that most Roman Catholics would now be aware that artificial contraception is deemed immoral by the magisterium. But if this is so, he said, must we conclude that all those who are practicing artificial contraception are, in fact, guilty of mortal sin? He thought not.

> A practical resolution of this problem lies, I think, in the distinction drawn by modern psychiatry between theoretical and evaluative knowledge. . . . The knowledge requisite for a mortal sin is not merely theoretical or speculative. It must be evaluative or appreciative. That is to say, a person must do more than know intellectually that a certain action is wrong. He [*sic*] must make this knowledge his own. He must personally perceive the moral good or evil involved in an action, so that he evaluates or appreciates it emotionally as well as in a purely abstract way. He must experience a certain emotional or affective revulsion from the evil, so that he can be said to feel as well as know that it is wrong.
>
> If in any situation a person lacks evaluative or appreciative knowledge of this sort, . . . he lacks the kind of knowledge that must be present for mortal sin.
>
> This, I would judge, is the condition of many Catholics at the present time. They are aware of the teaching of *Humanae Vitae.* But for a variety of reasons they are not able, at least for the present time, to personally appropriate as their own the values that it affirms.[2]

As far as I know, Dedek's analysis never received serious criticism, but his approach is also not often encountered. One suspects that it somehow strikes people as controversial, perhaps even eccentric. In fact, it is, as we saw in chapter 3, quite traditional. At the same time, when, in an insight firmly rooted in that tradition, a theologian like Dedek declares that to ground a genuine moral obligation a person "must experience a certain emotional or affective revulsion from the evil, so that he can be said to feel as well as know that it is wrong," he is using words that could as easily have been spoken by Antonio Damasio.

Charles Shelton, a psychologist who is both theologically literate and concerned about the issues of Christian ethics, also speaks in a way that is supportive of Damasio's view. Shelton speaks of empathy as "morality's heart."[3] He then goes on to declare that

> one of the most stimulating theories in recent developmental research is viewing morality as originating in the experience of emotion rather than cognition. . . . In regards to a morality of the heart, early emotions such as shame and guilt "inform" the heart. Such feelings are best expressed as *affective knowledge* that orients the heart to care and sensitivity.[4]

This integrated perspective finds a beautiful articulation in theologian Simon Harak's *Virtuous Passions*. Harak responds to what he views as a negative view of passion, proposing an alternative, very positive view. He then shows how the positive view is supported by the anthropology of Thomas Aquinas. Finally, Harak shows how the commitment to social justice demanded by the preaching of Jesus and the teachings of the church requires a "passion for justice."[5]

Finally, this perspective was articulated quite pointedly by theologian Daniel Maguire in his landmark book, *The Moral Choice*. The following comments will give a sense of Maguire's vision.

> Much influential thinking has been impaled on the fallacious dichotomy which divorces feeling from intelligence and affectivity from knowledge. It is my contention here that feeling is a knowing experience and that extreme mischief has been wrought, especially in ethics, by the failure to recognize this. Whether we take account of them or not, our feelings rise in the face of a morally adjudicable situation. And they do not arise as neutral outbursts, but as informed, evaluative reactions. Feelings may be mixed and contradictory just as abstract and intellectualized reasonings may be. Nevertheless, those feelings are a cognitive reaction, not a sideline eruption that takes place off the field, of knowing.[6]

> In moral knowledge, there is no purely emotional reaction and no purely conceptualized judgment. Conception and affection are essentially intertwined. Still, the distinction between the two is not a distinction without a difference. Affective knowledge is not the same as conceptualized knowledge. Abstract, conceptual knowledge can be distinguished from an affective and emotional response. The problem is that the distinction has been too drastically made and emotion has been considered something precognitive or pretercognitive. Affective knowing should be seen as a genuine though different kind of knowing. It calls for completion, and the mind should move on to other kinds of knowing to find that completion. Otherwise it will not be able ade-

quately to give reasons for its position. Neither will it know, without the intellectual work of comparison, whether its position is the result of bias or of genuine insight.[7]

Maguire's final comment provides an excellent angle on the true role of *cognitio speculativa.* This more analytic, abstract form of knowing is not the basis for actual moral choice. But it is the tool of analysis, wherein we can help to assess which items of *cognitio aestimativa* are rooted in accurate perceptions and which are rooted in bias. His comments also bring us to the final point of this chapter, a point that will open out into our ongoing discussion.

Conclusion

What is the source of our evaluative knowledge? The answer was implied in the analysis of Damasio. Our emotional reactions, said Damasio, are rooted in our dispositional representations. These, in turn, are rooted in past experiences, recorded in the images of memory. Maguire hints at the same answer when he admits that our affective responses represent a combination of bias and insight. In a word, our moral affections, our sensibilities involving both understanding and affection, are rooted in past experience. It is experience that is the ground of moral sensitivity. Put very simply, we morally respond in different ways because in the course of our lives we have been different places.

This insight was brought home to me forcefully when I once attended a lecture in which the speaker took a strong and controversial position. I could feel the tension in the audience, with some people rejoicing in the presentation, others rebelling against it. The lecture was to be followed by small group discussions, an interaction that could well have become most unpleasantly conflictual. But in introducing the discussion period, the master of ceremonies made an inspired contribution. He asked the audience to take out pieces of paper. Then he invited them to write down feelings they were having right at that moment. After a moment or so, he commented that feelings often are rooted in convictions; so he invited the audience to jot down the conviction behind each of their named feelings. Immediately the feelings had dignity, it seemed! Finally, the master of ceremonies commented that we were not born with those convictions, that they had developed over time. So he asked the participants to think of a life experience that had helped confirm that conviction within them. After a few moments, he suggested that the table discussion focus on this diversity of feelings, convictions, and, most especially, experiences. And what we discovered, of course, was that different feelings are rooted in different experiences. This is the homespun observation that is described by Maguire and explained by Damasio.

But if this observation is true, then the beginnings of a pastoral strategy already suggest themselves. If people who claim to be Christian do not regularly and spontaneously respond to moral dilemmas in a "Christ-like way," the solution lies in the introduction of additional experiences. The solution is not to be found in haranguing such people. Neither is it to be found in the dumping of painful guilt. On the contrary, the solution resides in allowing people the opportunity to experience situations from another point of view. These experiences will, in turn, affect the moral sensibilities, both immediately and also, by way of dispositional representations, in the future.

Much more needs to be said about this, however. The following chapters will address in detail the questions about how experiences shape our moral sensibilities, about where these experiences take place, about the dynamics of their development. And all of this, in turn, will increasingly suggest a pastoral strategy for the cultivation of Christian moral values.

Notes

1. Antonio Damasio, *Descartes' Error* (New York: G. P. Putnam's Sons, 1994).

2. John F. Dedek, "Humanae Vitae and the Confessor," *Chicago Studies* 7 (1968): 221–23.

3. Charles Shelton, *Morality of the Heart: A Psychology for the Christain Moral Life* (New York: Crossroad, 1990), 33.

4. Ibid., 74, 76.

5. Simon Harak, *Virtuous Passions: The Formation of Christian Character* (New York: Paulist Press, 1993).

6. Daniel Maguire, *The Moral Choice* (New York: Doubleday, 1978), 282.

7. Ibid., 285–86.

7

The Dynamics of Group Experience

THE LAST CHAPTER CONCLUDED WITH THE HOMESPUN OBSERVATION that moral sensibilities are shaped by experiences, that we feel differently because we've been different places. In this chapter I will amplify this observation in two ways. I will nuance the observation itself, and I will report a series of research findings that support that observation. In both cases, the goal will not be simply to add information indiscriminately (speculative knowledge!). Rather, it will be to gather information that is pertinent to our ministerial project, that suggests in a variety of ways initiatives that can help us become more successful in our efforts to "make disciples."

Kinds of Experiences

To begin, it may be helpful to distinguish two sorts of experiences: solitary and relational. By solitary experiences, I mean to identify things like sunsets and symphonies, art and technology, and to acknowledge their power to touch us and transform us. I mean to recognize the life-changing power that can come from witnessing an automobile accident or a birth, from a warm bath or a serious illness. All these involve "observations." But they are more than that; they deserve the name "experience." And as experiences, they influence and modify our sensibilities in ways that eventually affect our choices and our behavior.

But if some significant experiences are solitary, far more are relational. Human beings are social animals. Indeed, there is a sense in which it is accurate to say that we are never truly alone. Go for a "solitary" walk on the beach, and I wager that within minutes someone else will be "present" with you in your thoughts. These "others" may be friend or foe, but they will be present, generating a whole range of dispositional representations and the feelings that follow. Because of human consciousness, we are neverendingly connected to our fellow members of the human family. We are never really alone.

Thus, it is not surprising that many of our most significant experiences are relational. Consequently, it is by our experiences of and with other persons that our moral sensibilities are most decisively shaped. A wonderful, if simple, example of this is provided by the research of Elaine Hatfield and her colleagues, research that she aptly summarizes in the phrase, "emotional contagion."[1] Through an extensive series of experimental observations, Hatfield has tested and, it seems, verified a set of three propositions.

The first proposition declares that in conversation and interaction people tend automatically and continuously to mimic and synchronize their movements with the facial expressions, voices, postures, movements, and instrumental behaviors of others who are nearby. That is, if one person crosses his or her leg, it is very likely that others who are present will shortly do the same. If one person begins to talk more loudly, all will eventually increase the volume of their voices. If one person picks up a pencil or takes a drink from a coffee cup, others are likely to do the same.

The second proposition, extending this idea, declares that subjective emotional experiences are affected, moment to moment, by the activation of and/or feedback from such mimicry. Thus, for example, the raising of voices will, in turn, tend to make all the participants feel agitated, aggressive, perhaps even angry. Constant playing with pencils and such will, in turn, generate in the participants a feeling of boredom or lethargy. Leaning back in one's chair with legs crossed will stimulate a feeling of casual relaxation in all those involved.

This leads the researchers to a third proposition which serves as a summary: given the truth of propositions #1 and #2, one can assume that people tend to "catch" one another's emotions, moment to moment. Thus, a vivacious speaker not only entertains the audience; she or he stimulates in them the positive feelings that initially prompted the speaking style. And if one member of a group is depressed, the others are likely to be infected by the same feeling. So true is this, that a postulate of psychological counseling is that the therapist should take careful note of feeling states that seem to arise in herself or himself in the course of the counseling session. For these feelings within the therapist very likely mirror what the client is feeling, no matter what the client's words may declare.

A delightful example of this phenomenon was provided me by a pastoral minister. This woman felt that Sunday liturgy exhibited an unfortunately somber, unenthusiastic mood. She did not believe she could succeed in changing the presider's personal style, but wondered if she might make at least a small improvement on her own. Toward that end, she instructed the people who distributed Holy Communion to look at each recipient and smile. The result was beyond her wildest hopes! People smiled back, of course, but they also seemed to maintain the warm, friendly mood when they returned to their places. They produced significantly stronger emotional reactions to the announcements after communion, laughing responsively to comments made by the priest. And, perhaps most surprisingly, the music director noted that the congregation sang the closing song with verve and volume well beyond that of the previous musical moments. Something had changed, abidingly changed, through the chemistry of the smile. Emotional contagion had been manifested.

The Group

The observations of Hatfield and her colleagues point to a central truth: individuals are influenced by groups. So true is this that it may prove more accurate to say that particular value preferences are the possession of groups than that they are the possession of individuals. And if this is true, pastoral strategies for value preference modification will, of course, have to focus far more on groups than on individuals. But we are getting ahead of ourselves in naming this conclusion. Let's first explore this notion of the central role of the group.

One wag has commented that every adolescent is a psychologist; adolescents who are lucky enough to truly grow up, however, ultimately turn into sociologists! That is, in our early years we tend to focus on the power of the individual, on the pivotal value of autonomy. As we grow older, however, we come to realize how important groups are and how much they shape the individuals who belong to them. This is the insight of the mother who worries about the companions with whom her children "hang out." It is the wisdom of psychotherapists who, early in the counseling relationship, want to hear much about the client's "family of origin." It is the point of the Irish proverb that the apple does not fall far from the tree. And it is the sad knowledge of the teacher who understands that "one bad apple spoils the bushel" and that if the disruptive student is not removed from the class, the learning of the entire group will be undermined.

This truth explains the reason for a troubling but unavoidable fact: every group that takes itself seriously has a policy about excommunication. This term, loaded with unpleasant association for Catholics, may seem to name an aberration of communal life. But I think it does not. No doubt there are abuses of the power to exclude, abuses that are ultimately destructive of persons. But it is equally true that the group that stands for nothing ... ends up standing for nothing! So any group, a bowling league, a family, a church, that takes itself seriously has an implicit awareness that there are limits to the tolerable.

But please note: as this line of thinking implies, the limits set by groups do not express the line between good people and bad people. Rather they express the line between behavior, good or bad, that can be tolerated and behavior that, because it threatens the very existence of the group itself, must be prevented. Many forms of bad behavior do not threaten the life of the group; so they do not properly prompt the intervention known as excommunication. Thus, the act of excommunication is not a response to personal unworthiness; it is a response to communal danger.

Even the early church realized this. The writings of scriptures and of the early fathers condemn many forms of evil behavior. But only three sins prompted excommunication from the early church: adultery, homicide, and apostasy. Why is that? It seems the reason was that only these three acts directly threatened the life of the community and therefore the community's mission of preaching the gospel. Adultery, by intruding on the marital relationship, threatened the familial community. Homicide, by attacking the basic good of life, threatened the human community. And apostasy, by denying the core of the faith, threatened the faith community. These three sins, then, and not other offenses against sexuality or interpersonal rights or religious duty, required the communal response of exclusion.

Values, therefore, reside in groups as much as or more than they reside in individuals. This means that groups, like individuals, can be characterized as good or bad depending on the value preferences that they embrace. But it also means that, even when groups embrace good value preferences, they, like individuals, can be different from one another.

Every child can remember the first experience of entering another family's home and discovering that "they don't do it like us!" And every minister who has endeavored to provide cross-cultural service has been forced to face the same truth: different groups value things differently. Anglos and Hispanics often laugh about their respective stereotypical styles, offering comments that may contain a kernel of truth even as they also distort. Anglos say the Hispanics must work on the virtues of punctuality and dependability. Hispanics respond that Anglos need to improve their enactment of the virtues of compassion and hospitality. Similarly, ministers are often frustrated when the people they serve have values different from their own. What is more important: quiet reverence or social conviviality? Sexual control or exuberant relationality? Religious duty or communal involvement? All of these are good; everyone has a personal priority among the goods; and parishioners and ministers do not always share the same priorities. Therein lies the rub!

This idea of the group's power has been confirmed by social science research, notably by psychologist Norma Haan.[2] The theory of moral development constructed by Lawrence Kohlberg, which we considered in detail in chapter 4, is well known. In contrast to Kohlberg's view, Haan has developed a view of her own and has tested that view in a series of experiments.

Kohlberg's view, you will recall, understood moral development as synonymous with the development of moral *cognition*. That is, it is our ways of *understanding* morality that change over time; and these changes produce overall development. Kohlberg described the development as moving through six stages and proposed that the individual is propelled to a higher stage when she or he experiences *cognitive dissonance* between the views of the lower stage and some other moral intuitions.

Haan, on the other hand, understands moral development as represented by change in actual moral choices and moral action; and she views this development, which occurs in the course of life, as being on a continuum rather than in clearly demarcated stages.[3] Haan understands moral action as a process of *dialogue* involving the individual, other individuals and groups, the situation, and the moral dilemma. It is thus an intrinsically *social* process. She proposes further that the individual is propelled to a change in moral choice and moral action when he or she experiences *social dissonance* between the self and these valued others. As she puts it in one place:

The two systems [Kohlberg's and Haan's] agree that people must be dis-
equilibrated in order to develop (no one need cope when there are no
problems to face). But they differ as to the kind of conflict that is necessary. In the cognitive view the conflict is cognitive in nature; in the
interactional theory, threat or the actual experience of miscarried or
failed relations with others (the self's reactions to the self and the other,
the other's reactions to the self, and the other's reactions to him- or herself) constantly provide social disequilibrium.[4]

This is the view that Haan set out to test in a series of experiments
conducted at the University of California, Berkeley. Through adver-
tisements in campus newspapers and the like, she engaged fifteen
already existing, natural groupings of friends. After pretesting the
members of all the groups (119 individuals in all) both for their level
of cognitive moral thinking and for their skill in moral decision making, five of the groups participated in a series of meetings in which they
discussed cases of moral dilemmas, classic cases of the sort developed
by Kohlberg and his associates. These groups were thus encouraged to
experience and deal with cognitive dissonance. The other ten groups
played games that involved them in concrete projects requiring common and shared outcomes. For example, in one game the group was
told they were the last surviving members of the human race. Then,
over the period of time they were presented with several issues: for
example, whether to allow a possibly contaminated survivor to join
them, whether to help a member wishing to commit suicide, and so on.
Thus the process in these groups was designed to provide experiences
of social dissonance.

Despite the different focuses of the two sets of groups, both cognitive and social dissonance occurred in all groups. So Haan's process
involved two observers in every meeting, one each to look for cognitive and social dissonance, an arrangement that allowed for a rather
complex set of observations. Finally, after a series of several meetings,
followed by a month or more of no interactions, the 119 members were
post-tested, again for both cognitive approach and personal skill.
Although her conclusions are complicated, subtle, and nuanced,
indeed tentative, and can only be fully understood by reviewing the
publications mentioned here, a few points can be highlighted.

First, Haan found that "cognitive disequilibrium was consistently
more salient [i.e., common, measurable, notable, etc.] than social
disequilibrium in both discussion and game groups."[5] So in sheer
quantitative terms, there was more intellectual disagreement than

interpersonal conflict, and at first blush it seemed more significant. But for all that, it didn't seem to be very important. "Calculation of the effects for gaming versus discussing on the index of relative development showed, contrary to Kohlbergian curricular recommendations, that cognitive-moral development was significantly more accelerated by the experience of gaming than by discussing."[6] So even the *cognitive* development that Kohlberg intended to encourage occurred more rapidly and substantially as a result of group interactions than of the intellectual explorations recommended by him.

A similar conclusion was found when the researchers measured the participants' growth in the skill of choosing, deciding, and resolving conflicts. Though the *amount* of intellectual dissonance was greater, the *influence* of interpersonal dissonance was more significant. Indeed,

> cognitive disequilibrium was more pronounced than social disequilibrium whatever the group experience, but it had little or no effect on development in either moral system. On hindsight, we see that cognitive disequilibrium is part of *all* moral encounters that are not immediately resolved. But the present results remind us that a persistent or even salient feature of a phenomenon is not necessarily the cause of its development or change.[7]

At the same time, neither was it social disequilibrium alone that predicted the moral development of the individual. One other variable emerged and needed to be considered: the individual's ability to handle the conflict involved. When the conflict became overwhelming, leading the participant either to capitulate or to isolate, then little personal development took place. But when the participant had the personal resources such as ego strength and self-esteem to tolerate the conflict, then significant change occurred.

> Social disequilibrium did not in itself account for either cognitive or interactional development. This variable, which represented the reactions of groups, had to be brought into interaction with the individual students' characteristic strategies of handling conflict, before development was systematically predicted. . . . Two implications follow from this overall pattern of results: First, development seems to rise out of the emotional, interactive experience of moral-social conflict and not from the cognitive experience of finding that one's reasoning [is] in disagreement with another's higher stage thinking. . . . The second effective support of development in both moral systems was the characteristic way that individual students handled conflict. Their development seemed to depend on whether or not they cope function-

ally, that is allow themselves to recognize and tolerate conflict so that they could learn from it.[8]

Haan's research, then, shows the profoundly social character of moral development. The studies of sociologist Samuel Oliner point to the same conclusion. A few of his thoughts will prove helpful to us as we bring this discussion to an end.

Rescuers' Look

Samuel Oliner is a Jew who, as a small boy, escaped death in the Holocaust only because he was hidden by Christian neighbors. Now a sociologist teaching at Humboldt State University in California, Oliner has long wondered why these people risked their lives for him and why other Christians did or did not act similarly. To seek answers to his questions Oliner has led a major study. He located 682 authenticated rescuers, as he calls them, and 126 nonrescuers, people who either did nothing (bystanders) or who helped Jews in less specific ways (active nonrescuers). For research purposes the nonrescuers were matched with the rescuers in age, sex, education, and geographic location. Oliner also located and studied 150 rescued survivors, people like himself. His study included extensive interviews and the administration of a variety of psychological tests. Oliner has reported the results of this study in a fascinating book, *The Altruistic Personality,* coauthored with his wife.[9]

Perhaps Oliner's most fundamental conclusion is that the difference between rescuers and nonrescuers resides not in opportunity, finding oneself in a situation where it is possible to help, but in character, an ingrained tendency to help in whatever circumstances one encounters. But for our purposes, even more important are his answers to two subsequent questions. What elements of the characters of rescuers were different? And how did they come to have those different sorts of character?

When his subjects were invited to talk about the values expressed in their lives, values they had received from their parents, Oliner found no difference between rescuers and nonrescuers in the appeal to what he calls "equity values," such things as honesty, fair play, truthfulness. But he found a substantial difference in their tendency to speak of "care values," such things as generosity, concern, helpfulness. Forty-four percent of rescuers chose such words, compared to 25 percent of active nonrescuers and 21 percent of bystanders. What is more, rescuers also mentioned much more often the importance of extending one's care to all—"universality" as Oliner terms it. Thirty-nine percent of rescuers used this sort of language, as contrasted to 15 percent of active nonrescuers and 13 percent of bystanders. Finally,

> the ethical values of care and inclusiveness that distinguished rescuers were not merely abstract or philosophical preferences. Rather, they reflected a key dimension of rescuers' personalities—the way they characteristically related to others and their sense of commitment to them.[10]

This quality of involvement, of commitment to other people, Oliner terms "attachment."

But where do these things come from? How does it happen that some people develop personalities characterized by care, universality, and attachment? Oliner's research suggests an answer. And his words are so well chosen that I can only quote them.

> A critical influence on their development was the way in which their parents disciplined them.
>
> The extent to which discipline—from teaching to punishing—is a central focus of the parent–child interaction is probably vastly underrated as an influence on development. Some researchers estimate that beginning at age two, children are commonly pressured by parents to change their behaviors on the average of once every six or seven minutes. . . . The reasons for which compliance is requested and the modes through which it is elicited communicate profound and long-lasting messages about right and wrong and about desirable relationships. . . .
>
> Parents whose disciplinary techniques are benevolent, particularly those who rely on reasoning, are more likely to have kind and generous children. . . . Hoffman, who has done considerable research on discipline and prosocial behaviors, says that inductive reasoning is particularly conducive to altruism. Induction focuses children's attention on others' feelings, thoughts, and welfare. . . .
>
> Overall, significantly fewer rescuers recalled any controls imposed on them by the most intimate persons in their early lives. . . .
>
> Perhaps more important, parents of rescuers depended significantly less on physical punishment and significantly more on reasoning.[11]

So Oliner's research confirmed these insights of Hoffman, that adults whose character is defined by care, universality, and attachment are people who, as children, were disciplined through a technique known as "induction," the combination of strong expectations with clear explanations.

This combination of expectation and explanation, then, is a pivotal component of a strategy designed to inculcate values. The making of disciples requires both.

Norms of the Group

One last element of Oliner's presentation will assist us. Imagine that we pose to our population of rescuers the following question: Why did you do it? Oliner has already organized their responses in terms of references to "equity values" and "care values," and has reported that the latter sort are much more common in this group. Now he offers another way of sorting his respondents' answers, using categories developed by sociologist Janusz Reykowski. As Oliner summarizes Reykowski's views, some people explain their behavior by appeal to their feelings, to *empathy:* "I was moved by their plight." Others appeal to *group norms:* "That's the way we do things." And yet others appeal to *principles:* "That is just how people ought to act."

Sorting through the responses of his population of rescuers, Oliner made a surprising discovery. Only 11 percent explained their behavior on grounds of principle. This is particularly intriguing since principled judging and acting are what Lawrence Kohlberg proposed as the ideal of moral development. Of course, one could simply argue that these people were not particularly developed from a moral point of view. But given their actions, that is an embarrassing interpretation: you're liable to be more virtuous if you're less ethically developed! Another possible interpretation is that Kohlberg is simply wrong. We will return to this idea shortly.

By contrast, 37 percent of the rescuers offered explanations for their behavior that utilized the language of compassion. But most significantly, 52 percent used the language of group norms![12] Here we are not talking about the sort of legalism that holds persons captive, that dominates and dehumanizes them. Rather, we are talking about shared norms of behavior in which a person is freely invested and which come from group identity. It is as if the participants are saying: "This is my group. I choose to be part of this group, I cannot imagine myself being otherwise. And I know that we, as a group, have particular ways of behaving. So these are my ways of behaving also."

Two concluding comments can be drawn from this data. First, it is clear that the rescuers behaved as they did in these particular circumstances because it was their characteristic way of behaving in every circumstance. As Oliner declares, their responses were less explicit conscious choices than characteristic ways of attending to routine events. . . . Many rescuers themselves reflected this view, saying that they "had no choice" and that their behavior deserved no special attention, for it was simply an "ordinary" thing to do.[13]

What is more, this characteristic way of acting was developed as part of the development of a personal identity intertwined with a group identity, where both were influenced by inductive approaches to childhood discipline.

Second, the resulting vision of and approach to life are appropriated by the person in a manner far more emotional than rational. "While they may articulate such standards as cognitive principles, they experience them viscerally."[14] And, as mentioned above, if this approach is presented not only as actual fact but also as theoretical ideal, it diverges significantly from the view proposed by Lawrence Kohlberg, where cognitive development is recommended. In this regard one is reminded of the critiques of Kohlberg by Carol Gilligan and others,[15] speculating that he was infected by a sort of gender bias. Perhaps the focus on cognitive development represents a culturally based ideal of manliness, perhaps even of post-enlightenment maleness!

And perhaps, as we considered in our discussion of the work of Antonio Damasio and as Norma Haan has argued quite explicitly, the problem is even more fundamental. Perhaps by confusing moral knowing with moral choosing, Kohlberg simply and utterly misunderstands the situation of human acting. Perhaps people live, and should live, not out of their principles but out of their relationships, especially those forged early in life but also those developed through the years. No doubt relationships can be stifling and destructive. But in that case, is the solution to escape from relationships into principles or to compensate for bad relationships in good relationships? And if the solution is the latter, then perhaps the role of reason is not to craft the principles out of which one logically lives but to organize and articulate the development of relational life so that it can be nurtured so that, in the end, this fabric of life-giving, freely-embraced group norms can come to ground a life.

It is the group, then, that is the home of values. And if this is true, then the making of disciples may really be a process of creating communities of discipleship, homes where the value priorities of the disciple flourish. The next chapter will explore this theme in increasing detail.

Notes

1. Elaine Hatfield, John T. Cacioppo, Richard L. Rapson, *Emotional Contagion* (Cambridge: Cambridge University Press, 1994).

2. Norma Haan, Elaine Aerts, Bruce A. B. Cooper, *On Moral Grounds* (New York: New York University Press, 1985); Norma Haan, "Processes of Moral Development: Cognitive or Social Disequilibrium?" *Developmental Psychology* 21 (1985): 996–1008; see also Mark Poorman, *Interactional Morality* (Washington, D.C.: Georgetown University Press, 1993), which includes a detailed examination of Haan's work.

3. These two points, the focus on choice and the rejection of "stage thinking," also characterize the position of Craig Dykstra, *Vision and Character* (New York: Paulist Press, 1981). Dykstra, however, defends his position with logical argument rather than with social science research as does Haan.

4. Haan et al., *On Moral Grounds,* 65–66.

5. Haan, "Processes of Moral Development," 1000.

6. Ibid.

7. Ibid., 1004.

8. Ibid., 1005.

9. Samuel P. Oliner and Pearl M. Oliner, *The Altruistic Personality* (New York: Free Press, 1988); see also Morton Hunt, *The Compassionate Beast* (New York: Doubleday Anchor, 1990), which includes an extensive discussion of Oliner's work as well as many other useful insights.

10. Ibid., 171.

11. Ibid., 178–79.

12. Ibid., 221.

13. Ibid., 221–22.

14. Ibid., 250.

15. Carol Gilligan, *In a Different Voice: Psychological Theory and Women's Development* (Cambridge, Mass.: Harvard University Press, 1982).

8

The Chemistry of Relationship

Q: I have been watching the latest TV commercials . . . which encourage adolescent girls to postpone sex until they are married. The ads are well done, but I wonder: Will they have an impact on teenagers? . . . .

A: Probably not. "Ads on teen pregnancy and premarital sex have a marginal impact," says Father Andrew M. Greeley. . . . "What *does* have an impact is their parents—not what they say but the example they set."[1]

THIS COLLOQUIAL REPORT, TAKEN FROM A NEWSPAPER, SUMMARIZES a critical insight confirmed by both common sense and careful research. Father Greeley has been trumpeting for years the research findings that confirm this idea, and the scholarly contributions of many have helped to highlight it. This chapter will describe the insight in a general way and then consider two important scholarly works.

What is the central insight? Put simply, it is that people are influenced by one another and that, in particular, people are influenced by the significant others in their lives. Greeley states this insight in his clear declaration that parents, especially in their actual behavior, exercise serious influence on their children. But this influence is not limited to parents. Rather, it is a permanent dimension of human life. So let us explore this insight.

We can begin with a simple question: What is the goal of childhood? Without thinking, one might be tempted to respond: The goal of childhood is to be a happy child! But I suspect that this is not the case. Those of us who are fans of the late lamented cartoon *Calvin and Hobbes* realize that a key to its humor was Calvin's dissatisfaction with the status quo; he simply did not like being a child! And the same thing seems true of all children. Indeed, it is probably the case that no child is truly happy, for the simple reason that children are small and big people run the world. Hence, the goal of childhood is not to be a happy child; it is to be a happy grown-up. In service to that goal, then, children are endlessly alert, searching for happy grown-ups. And when they find one, they tend to draw an obvious conclusion: "Maybe I should live like that person. Their way of life has made them happy; perhaps it will make me happy too."

Children are involved, then, in a never-ending process of observation and imitation. And not just children. Consider the amusing observation that all of us have one thing in common: no matter what age we are, we are all this age for the very first time. Hence, we are all equally incompetent at being the age we are! That is, there is a perpetual edge of newness to life, a sense that one is encountering new challenges, that old solutions may no longer be adequate to the moment. And how do we cope with this edge? We do what we did as children: we watch other people like hawks! We indulge in the act of observation, with an openness to the act of imitation. And through that mechanism of observation and imitation we seek to deal with the ongoing but ever new challenges of human living, hoping thereby to achieve that happiness which remains our lifelong personal goal.

Mentoring

This homespun observation, true of children and true also of adults, has been confirmed in the careful research of social science scholars. Let's begin with the findings of Daniel Levinson. In chapter 4 we have already explored Levinson's discovery that adult life is broken into a series of stages, with substantial periods of interstage flux. Now we turn to another of his discoveries: the mentoring relationship.

In his book *Seasons of a Man's Life,* Levinson reported the results of his study of a group of adult males.[2] One of his findings was that every one of the men in his study reported having had an important relationship in the early adult years, between the ages of about eighteen and thirty. This relationship joined the young man to a somewhat older person, about eight to fifteen years his senior. The older person Levinson termed a "mentor," and in this context the younger person acted as a "protégé." In Levinson's sample all the mentors were men, but he does not believe it essential that this be a same-sex relationship. Indeed, he refers to cases where women, perhaps because of a shortage of female mentors, report important mentoring relationships with men. There is no reason to presume that the same is not possible in cases involving female mentors and male protégés.

In any case, the nature of this relationship and the role of the mentor are consistent: he or she is a person who introduces the protégé into adult life, "shows him or her the ropes," and perhaps actually facilitates entrance into the adult world through sponsorship, introductions, and referrals. The mentoring relationship is, in a word, a functional, utilitarian relationship. But for all that, it also operates much like a friendship in that the age closeness makes the mentor and protégé more like peers than like parent and child. In fact,

> the mentor represents a mixture of parent and peer; he must be both and not purely either one. If he is entirely a peer, he cannot represent the advanced level toward which the younger man is striving. If he is very parental, it is difficult for both of them to overcome the generational difference and move toward the peer relationship that is the ultimate (though never fully realized) goal of the relationship.[3]

As observed by Levinson, the mentoring relationship serves a variety of functions. And inasmuch as many of them represent obvious needs, it is generally a quite explicit, intentional relationship. But it also has one function that is often not so explicit. One of the characteristics of early adulthood is the creation and affirmation of a "dream" for one's adulthood. In this regard it is a critical function of the mentor to validate that dream, to confirm for the protégé both the value and the realism of the dream, and perhaps even to expedite its realization through helpful interventions.

For all these positive characteristics, the mentoring relationship has a dark side too. "Mentoring is best understood as a form of love relationship. [Like all such relationships, then,] it is difficult to terminate in a reasonable, civil manner."[4] Yet terminate it must, for the protégé must in the end become an adult in his or her own right. She or he must move beyond whatever notes of apprenticeship were involved in the relationship, to accept final responsibility for the self and, in all likelihood, to make personal choices without the mentor's blessing and maybe over the mentor's objection. In line with this idea, Levinson reports that mentoring relationships last, on average, two to three years and rarely over a decade. And while they sometimes evolve into genuinely peer-type friendships, they more often end on a note of conflict or acrimony.

Finally, Levinson observes that, as one might expect given the note of apprenticeship in the mentoring relationship, such relationships are almost never found in people's lives after the age of thirty or so. Thus, mentoring, as Levinson defines it, is a specific, focussed example of that more general pattern, the life activity of observation and imitation, which we described above.

Reflections on Mentoring

It is a powerful example, to be sure. Most of us can probably recall individuals who functioned as mentors in our lives. Listening to Levinson's description gives us an opportunity to celebrate the gift that was involved in such relationships, perhaps even to express gratitude to the one who served as mentor. At the same time, coming to understand the typically troubled end of mentoring relationships may provide some consolation if such was the case for us. Levinson's observations imply, and there seems no reason to deny, that there is nothing wrong with moving on, becoming one's own person. Indeed, such a move may be critical to the achievement of full adult maturity. But there is surely a price to be paid. Perhaps listening to Levinson provides an opportunity for grieving what may have been inevitable but was, for all that, also sad.

Levinson's observations may also touch us if we are old enough to have served as mentors. It is a complex relationship. On the one hand, it is satisfying to the ego to be so appreciated by a younger person, to be sought for counsel and assistance. At the same time, it is painful to find requests for reciprocity unfulfilled, to discover that the protégé is, indeed, going to move on. Teachers often talk about the asceticism of their work, of the tremendous importance of maintaining peer relationships outside the school setting lest the students become too important, and of the inevitable price of the caring, no matter how carefully it is done.

But if the relationships described and analyzed by Levinson provide us with a powerful example of the perennial human dynamic of observation and imitation, they are nonetheless only an example. Children evidently indulge in observation and imitation long before they enter the particular relationship that Levinson calls mentoring. And reflection on one's experience, on the never-ending edge of newness in life and on the consequent effort to find the key to living well the next stage of one's life, suggests that the dynamic continues after the moment of mentoring is past. This abiding dimension of human life has been studied and described in helpful ways by social psychologist Albert Bandura.

Modeling

Bandura is considered a leading exponent of "social learning theory," a psychological approach that seeks to explain how persons learn behaviors and values and that focuses on the role of social forces in that learning. He had developed ground-breaking ideas in this field as far back as 1963 and has continued to contribute through more recent important books.[5] He has also been the subject of extensive discussions on the part of other scholars.[6]

In developing his theory of social learning, Bandura became convinced of a central role in the process of human learning played by a process that he called "modeling." Modeling (unlike mentoring) is not necessarily a conscious process. The term does not describe something one sets out to do, as one might set out to offer good example. Rather, it describes a fundamental fact of human life: that we cohabit the universe, that we inevitably live in one another's presence, and that, as a result, we are continually involved in a process of observation and imitation. Indeed, these two terms, which I have already used in this chapter, come from Bandura.

> For Bandura and [his colleague Richard] Walters imitation was elevated to a position of central importance. . . . They documented that observational learning occurs even when a model's responses are not reproduced during acquisition and, therefore, could receive no reinforcement [which others had argued was the pivotal factor. Thus] . . . they moved observational learning into primary position among learning mechanisms, arguing that it was a much more efficient technique of behavior change than either direct learning or successive approximation.[7]

So in this regard Bandura is offering scientific corroboration of our homespun reflection on the dynamic whereby persons take on particular approaches to human living: it is a process of observation and imitation. But Bandura's contribution is not just confirmatory. His research also offers us several detailed comments that go beyond our initial reflection. For one thing, Bandura's research led him to the conclusion that for observational learning to take place successfully, four things are necessary. It will be worth considering each of these conditions one by one.

First, the learner must pay attention to the behavior he or she is meant to observe. In our world of sensory overload, this is no mean feat. Christian preachers often grieve over the burden of trying to compete on Sunday morning with the motion picture the congregation has attended on Saturday evening. The glazed look in the eyes of many worshipers suggests that we do not have their attention. Bandura says quite clearly: if we do not have their attention, we will not change their behavior.

Second, successful observational learning requires that the observed behavior be retained in the learner's memory. To some extent this comment merely explains the necessary "natural" substratum for learning. If the severely handicapped find it more difficult to learn, one of the reasons for the difficulty is their inability to retain in memory the alternatives that experience proposes. But the comment also has implications for all of us. For one thing, it means that efforts must be made to focus the observation for the learner, taking steps to assure that it is retained in a clear and nuanced way. For another thing, it suggests that we can facilitate social learning whenever we nurture human capacities for imaginative remembering. Basic educational strategies can thus make a difference in people's abilities to learn from experience and to benefit from the dynamic called modeling.

Third, the learner must in fact perform the imitation. That is, to assure ongoing imitation, one must start with initial imitation. Yes, even in the most sophisticated psychological theory of development, the place of "practice" is protected. If practice does not perhaps make perfect, it at least makes possible!

Finally, the learner must be motivated to imitate the observed behavior. That is, the behavior must somehow strike the learner as attractive, as desirable. That is why children in the mold of comic book character Calvin imitate those happy grown-ups. Perhaps this is also why parishioners tend not to imitate sour or depressed preachers of the so-called good news. But most cases are far more complicated than this. How do we communicate the desirability of a life-style of fidelity and sacrifice, especially when those very behaviors led the savior to the cross and when they have done the same for countless followers through the ages? There are possible answers to this question. The observed fact that living this way gives some people a sense of joy and peace that is thrilling if not contagious: this is one answer. A vision of life that holds out opportunities for happiness that transcend the here-

and-now: this is another. But there is no denying that the question is important.

So Bandura clarifies the conditions for successful observational learning: attention, memory, action, and motive. One more factor strikes me as important, even though it is discussed elsewhere rather than as a member of this list of conditions. This factor is highlighted in Bandura's term "self-efficacy."

> According to [Bandura's statement of] self-efficacy theory, people develop domain-specific beliefs about their own abilities and character-istics that guide their behavior by determining what they try to achieve and how much effort they put into their performance in that particular situation or domain.[8]

In other words, the effort people put into a project is dependent on whether they really, truly believe they can achieve the goal. One can pair up a student who has academic difficulties with the brightest person in the class, and observational learning will not take place. For the "plugger" will be hobbled by the realization (perhaps true, in this case) that imitation will never produce the behaviors which the model exhibits.

If this judgment of adequacy is accurate, then it is surely helpful. For it prevents people from wasting time in unrealistic imitation and being disappointed by useless efforts. But if the judgment is erroneous, the result of a deficit in self-esteem, for example, rather than of accurate self-understanding, then it is sadly destructive. And conversely, if the misjudgment can be overcome, then outstanding success (rooted in intense and focussed effort) is possible. One thinks of the movie *Stand and Deliver*, which told the story of a mathematics teacher in a high school serving an impoverished area of Los Angeles. He convinced a group of students, over their objections and the objections of many people around them, that they could master advanced, college-level calculus. And in the end they did.

This dependence on self-efficacy is confirmed by Bandura's research. It is also, I suspect, confirmed by common experience. And so we can now say that successful modeling is dependent on five factors: attention, memory, action, motivation, and personal believability. It is when these five conditions are fulfilled that the process of observation and imitation, that phenomenon called observational learning, takes place. It is when these conditions are fulfilled—and when a model of genuine discipleship is present—that efforts at the making of disciples will succeed.

Summary

These insights from social psychology have been ably summarized by the writer Morton Hunt in his intriguing book *The Compassionate Beast.* Having presented a wide array of research and having delightfully embellished it with many anecdotes, Hunt summarizes his view of the process by which values are transmitted. As he reads the literature, Hunt sees six factors.

First and foremost, there is the relationship between a child and its parents. Not that initial family experiences cannot be transcended. But they are never forgotten, and their influence is probably never completely eliminated. Second, says Hunt, come the many other examples of modeling that occur in one's life. And in developing this point, he is obviously proclaiming the kind of insights we have already discovered in the research of Bandura.

Third, and in some ways raising quite a different angle, there is the experience of discipline and training. But when Hunt explicates this item, it turns out that he is not denying his previous points, only nuancing them.

> Power assertion and love withdrawal often produced the desired behavior but not character changes. The children complied reluctantly and with anger, anxiety, or guilt, but without internalizing the parents' (and thus society's) norms. Induction, on the other hand, especially by warm and loving parents not only yielded the desired behavior but an awareness of others' feelings and needs, and began the internalizing of the parents' and society's standards.[9]

So Hunt is confirming the research of Oliner: expectation plus explanation results in internalization of desired behavior.

Fourth, Hunt notes the significance of labeling, the process by which we name people in such a way that they tend to shape their behavior out of the named identity. Obviously, this insight is a two-edged sword. The labeling that affirms ("You are a good person. Even my complaint is rooted in my knowledge that you are capable of more.") can call forth the best within persons. But the labeling that condemns ("You are a jerk!") can have the opposite effect. So labeling is a tool to be handled gingerly.

Fifth, says Hunt, personal formation is aided by mere repetition. "Learning by doing," as he calls it, has long been a component of education. Recent emphases upon more subtle techniques have sometimes seemed to suggest that rote learning and simple enactment are without effect. This is not the case. As Hunt reports,

> in various experiments in which children have been persuaded to give part of their winnings in a game to unnamed poor children, to write letters to children in hospitals, and to help a teacher pick up spilled cards or paper clips, they later were readier to help and more generous with their help than comparable children who had not had such experiences.[10]

Finally, in a declaration that seems to me to summarize all that has preceded it, Hunt proclaims the central significance of social interaction, of the multiplicity of experiences, observations, and relationships that comprise a life, in the shaping of a person's character. Indeed, it is important to remember that, even as we attempt to be more intentional about providing positive experiences to those we seek to influence, no one can ever control the full range of experiences to which others are exposed. So there always remains the possibility that some other experiences, more negative than those we offer, will finally prove more influential in the lives of those we serve and love. We can, in the end, only offer and commend, we cannot ever compel, the appropriation of virtue.

Sociological Perspectives

In exploring the ways in which individuals and groups interact, we have been delving into a field known as social psychology. For the most part, we have been entering that field through its psychological door, inasmuch as both Levinson and Bandura are psychologically trained. Before we conclude this discussion a brief foray into more sociologically oriented contributions, developing two sets of ideas, will prove helpful.

As a general rule, most people presume that sociology is interested in the shape and dynamics of large groups—cities, schools, extended families, and the like—whereas psychology focuses on individuals. In general this is true. But almost since the beginning of the science, some sociologists have been interested in how the behavior and attitudes of individuals are affected by the groups that surround them and, indeed, by all their interpersonal experiences. A school of thought within sociology that addresses these concerns is "symbolic interactionism."[11]

This obscure title actually says something very important for our project. Symbolic interactionists assert that individuals are shaped by their interactions—a not surprising position for a sociologist to take! But this view is nuanced in two critical ways. First, proponents of this view do *not* view the individual as the passive recipient of the interactional experience, people who are inevitably shaped by particular circumstances. No, they also energetically affirm the power of the individual to "decide" what to make of the experiences. Rather cleverly, they affirm this "autonomy" without undermining their initial conviction about the power of interaction by saying that individuals also engage in *self-interaction*. That is, people "dialogue" with themselves, and in this dialogue they decide what to "make" of their interactions with others. So on the one hand, there are certain determined factors in human development, for I have only the actual experiences of my life to respond to. On the other hand, there is a note of genuine freedom, for I retain the capacity, in internal dialogue, to "say" what these experiences will mean to me.

Second, these sociologists nuance their view of interactions by asserting that these interactions are highly symbolic in nature. In our interactions with the worlds both of persons and of things, we do not encounter simple "reality." Rather, we always encounter reality that has meaning. But the meanings are multiple, and in this regard they are intrinsically symbolic. The same piece of wood may, in some circumstances, be a club; in others, a wand of authority; and in others, a tool for hitting a home run! Thus, George Herbert Mead, one of the pivotal figures in symbolic interactionism, distinguished between "things," reality in its mere facticity, and "objects," reality invested with meaning by the agent, symbolic reality.[12]

The problem, of course, is that different people invest the same things with different symbolic meanings, so that they are really different objects. The tremendous challenge of cross-cultural activities is trying to understand the meaning that things have in profoundly different settings. But symbolic interactionism extends this notion, to remind us that everything has at least slightly different symbolic meaning for each of us, even if, in a general way, we come from similar cultural settings. Hence, a permanent component of care for the other is the effort to discern the way in which a particular "thing" is an "object" for the person I seek to serve.

Symbolic interactionism offers another angle, then, on our basic claim that moral development occurs in a process of observation and imitation. It does affirm that claim, and affirms it with a vengeance.

> Not only do "things" acquire meanings through ongoing activity, so do people. . . . In other words, we come to know who and what we are through interactions with others. We become objects to ourselves by attaching to ourselves symbols that emerge from our interaction with others, symbols having meanings growing out of that interaction. As any other symbols, self symbols have action implications: they tell us (as well as others) how we can be expected to behave in our ongoing activity.[13]

But symbolic interactionism notes that the same "observed thing" may really mean different things and that we cannot altogether control what it will mean. And it reminds us that, in the end, the individual will enter a self-interaction in which he or she will decide what meaning it will have in this case. Thus, the process called modeling, central as it is, is not in any way automatic or uncomplicated. On the contrary, it is complex and finally ambiguous.

A second set of ideas, emerging from contemporary sociology and serving our project, has become known as "identity theory,"[14] "which is in part a refinement and in part an extension of the traditional symbolic interactionist perspective."[15]

This theory combines and connects three ideas. First there is "identity," which is understood as "role identity." That is, given the bias of sociologists that the group is centrally important to the shaping of individuals, those who work in identity theory take as a given that we *are* our roles. And I think it is fair to say that, at least to a large extent, their conviction matches our experience. People don't simply say, "I raised a child." Rather, they say, "I *am* a parent." To some extent at least, I *am* the roles I embrace. At the same time, I operate in many different settings. So I have—and I am—several different roles, and not just one. Thus, even in my role identity, I am complex.

Second, these authors speak of "identity salience." "Salience," a rather obscure word, is roughly synonymous with "significance" or "centrality" or "importance." That is, of the many identities I have, some are more significant or central than others. My identity, for example, as a teacher, may be more "salient" for me than my identity as a dweller on Hood Avenue. For someone else, however (say, a homemaker all of whose time is spent on Hood Avenue), the latter identity might be highly salient.

Finally, identity theory speaks of "commitment." Please note: the theory uses this word in a rather unusual way. Roughly synonymous with "locked in," commitment refers to the experience of necessity. For example, in aeronautics, airplane pilots refer to the point on a runway where they are "committed to a take-off," that is, the point where there is literally "no turning back." Similarly, in the sociological literature called identity theory, commitment refers to what happens when one's set of relationships (and therefore one's self-worth and security) *depends* on one having a particular role. And it is a matter of degree. That is, the more relationships I have that depend on my being a teacher, the more I am committed to that identity. And the *more important* to me the relationships that depend on my being a teacher, the more committed I am.

Now we can summarize identity theory itself. It is a theory that declares the following: the greater the commitment involved in a particular identity, the more salient that identity will be. And the more salient an identity is, the more likely that role related behaviors consistent with the identity will take place.[16] Or, to put this a bit more accessibly, the more that my relationships depend on my having a particular role, the more that role will be central to me. And the more a particular role is central to me, the greater the likelihood that in role-related settings I will behave in accord with that role.

As you may have noticed in this presentation, proponents of identity theory limit their claim. They specify that they are talking about "role-related behaviors." That is, in the privacy of one's home one may behave inconsistently. Or in one's fantasy, one may imagine another way of behaving. Or in settings where the role in question isn't relevant, one may behave differently. But at least in cases where one's role is truly pertinent, the causal chain, commitment-salience-behavior, seems to describe the truth. And even with this limitation in its application, this theory is saying something important.

Think, if you will, about the (stereotypical) priest who cannot resign from the ministry until his mother dies. Think of married persons who postpone divorce until the children are grown. Or what do you make of the man I once met, a scientist who assured me that salt had no influence on high blood pressure and who then mentioned, almost accidentally, that he "just happened" to be employed by a salt manufacturer? Yes, proponents of identity theory are saying something important. It may not be the only truth, but it is a valuable insight. People's behavior is ultimately influenced by the number and importance of the relationships whose continuance depends on their embracing the role that the behavior enacts.

Conclusion

Ministers, for example, intend to call people to a life of discipleship. They want the members of the community to live out the role of disciple in all the myriad behaviors that may express that role. Identity theory invites us to realize that people will in fact behave in this way to the extent that the role of disciple is salient for them. That is, in the first place the theory tells us it really is not a matter of behavior; it's a matter of role identity. So ministers have the job of inculcating an identity. And it tells us that it is not simply a matter of identity; it's a matter of identity *centrality*. Ministers have the job of encouraging the salience of the identity of disciple.

Second, identity theory invites us to realize that the salience of a particular identity depends on the number and importance of the relationships whose continuation depends on it. So ministers are not simply in the identity-inculcation business. Rather, and more fundamentally, they are in the important-relationship-cultivation business. To the extent that relationships are truly valuable to a person and to the extent that the continuation of those relationships depends on my embracing a particular identity, to that extent I will tend to make that identity my own. And to the extent that the identity is mine, and central to me, to that extent I will behave in accord with it.

Ministry is a process of helping relationships to grow, relationships with other disciples and relationships with God's own self. This insight is surely not new, but it is important. And the developers of identity theory help us to appreciate its significance once more.

Transition

With these sociological reflections, part 2 of our project comes to an end. A few words summarizing our present position will help us transition into the next set of questions.

Our goal is to understand the "making of disciples." How do people come to embrace the values out of which they live? And knowing this, how might we be more effective in leading them to embrace the values of the gospel?

We began our social scientific consideration of these questions by realizing that we are talking not so much about value election as about value preference. The challenge is to encourage people to habitually and skillfully prefer certain values to others, certain ways of behaving to others. We then noted that these value preferences are profoundly affective in nature. They are not so much well thought out intellectual positions as they are evaluative appreciations. And in the third place, we came to understand that these affective preferences are rooted in the concreteness of our life experiences, that we choose differently because we've been different places in life.

But experiences, we saw, are social realities, since one way or another we live our entire lives in groups. And so we explored at great length the dynamics of group life. In reviewing the research of Hatfield, we noted the patterns of contagion that characterize groups. And in learning of Haan's experiments at the University of California, we discovered the power of group cohesion. Levinson led us to an appreciation of the role of the mentor, and Bandura helped us realize the abiding significance of modeling. Finally, we found that the world of relationship is a world of symbolic interactions. But we also found that it was a world of power. For identity theory showed us how much our behavior is controlled by our roles, which are, in turn, controlled by the relationships on which we depend for nurturance, meaning, and security.

The significance of experience is, then, hard to exaggerate. Even more will we find this to be true when we discover that the word "experience" covers arenas to which we have given almost no attention. Hard as it may be to imagine, the entire line of inquiry that has occupied us in this second part of our project represents only one dimension of experience. Now, we must turn to the other dimension of experience, not denying anything said thus far, but amplifying and enriching it with insights from very different sources.

In part 3, then, we turn to the other venue of experience.

Notes

1. *Parade* [as distributed by the *Chicago Tribune*] (July 14, 1996): 2.

2. Daniel Levinson, *Seasons of a Man's Life* (New York: Alfred A. Knopf, 1978). This work was popularized by Gail Sheehy, *Passages: Predictable Crises of*

Adult Life (New York: Dutton, 1976). Sheehy's more recent work can be found in *New Passages: Mapping Lives Across Time* (New York: Random House, 1995).

3. Levinson, *Seasons,* 99.

4. Ibid., 100.

5. Albert Bandura and R. H. Walters, *Social Learning and Personality Development* (New York: Holt, Rinehart & Winston, 1963); Albert Bandura, *Social Foundations of Thought and Action: A Social Cognitive Theory* (Englewood Cliffs, N.J.: Prentice Hall, 1986).

6. I particularly note Joan E. Grusec, "Social Learning Theory and Developmental Psychology: The Legacies of Robert Sears and Albert Bandura," *Developmental Psychology* 28 (1992): 776–86. My summary of Bandura's thought is dependent on Grusec's overview.

7. Grusec, "Social Learning Theory," 781.

8. Ibid., 782.

9. Morton Hunt, *The Compassionate Beast* (New York: Doubleday Anchor, 1990), 112.

10. Ibid., 115.

11. This summary is primarily based on the presentation found in Ruth A. Wallace and Alison Wolf, *Contemporary Sociological Theory*, 3rd edition (Englewood Cliffs, N.J.: Prentice Hall, 1991), 235–88. Another excellent summary may be found in Sheldon Stryker and Richard T. Serpe, "Commitment, Identity Salience, and Role Behavior: Theory and Research Example," in *Personality, Roles, and Social Behavior,* ed. William Ickes and Eric Knowles (New York: Springer-Verlag, 1982), 201–5, to which further reference will be made below.

12. Wallace and Wolf, *Contemporary Sociological Theory*, 243.

13. Stryker and Serpe, "Commitment," 202.

14. The ideas summarized here are taken from Stryker and Serpe, "Commitment," 199–218.

15. Ibid., 200.

16. See ibid., 207–8.

PART 3

THE OTHER VENUE

OF EXPERIENCE

Fingernails scraping on blackboard.

The long green snake

slithered through the garden,

and crept past the hammock

where I was peacefully dozing.

Lightning,

then—an instant later—

a deafening crash of thunder.

9

The Power of Imagination

AS YOU READ THE SENTENCES ON THE PREVIOUS PAGE, DID they provoke any reaction within you? A significant proportion of readers are likely to answer yes to this question. In fact, the reaction may have been quite dramatic: a shiver running down the spine, a bitter cold sweat across the brow, a skipped heartbeat. Indeed, a blood pressure cuff might well have recorded a momentary rise in the pressure. An EEG might well have indicated a spike of electrical activity in the brain.

And all this in spite of a simple fact: in the "real world" nothing happened!

Ah, the power of imagination. The human imagination is an extraordinary thing, able to generate powerful experiences, able to retrieve moving moments. So it will not be surprising to realize that imagination has an important role to play in the transmission of moral values. In one sense we have already encountered this insight. In chapter 6 we explored the research of Antonio Damasio. One of Damasio's key points is that memories are stored within the brain in the form of images or, as he called them, dispositional representations. Or to put this the other way around: dispositional representations are nothing else than past experiences as they survive within the brain.

Thus, for our present purposes, we can begin with this simple truth identified by Damasio: imagination is rooted in life experience. This is, of course, both good and bad news. Any careful analysis of the notion of conscience reminds us that moral sensibilities can be either accurate or inaccurate, well-formed or mis-formed. And the reason for this, we know, is the different life experiences a particular person uses as the basis for moral conviction. Still, it is the truth. Invite a group of individuals to close their eyes and to allow their imaginations to react freely. Then call out a series of evocative words: . . . peaceful . . . frightening . . . friend . . . enemy. . . . In all likelihood, every one of the individuals will have a quite specific picture that they associate with each word. And, in subsequent conversation, they will be able to tell you a great deal about that picture—what it refers to, what experience served as its source and explanation. Throughout it all, they will make clear the fact that imagination is rooted in experience.

But there is another side to this as well. Imagination is also the "second venue for experience." That is, imagination actually precipitates experience; or, to say it more accurately, experience takes place just as really in the imagination as it does in the so-called real world. This is what we are taught by the visceral reaction to the sentences that began this chapter, and in recent research, a much fuller appreciation of this fact has been developing.

I am told of an athletic coach, working with a high school basketball team. He utilized all the customary tools in the training of his team: exercise, practice, instruction. But he also utilized another tool. "Every night, when you go to bed," he said, "last thing you do, turn out the light, close your eyes, and take fifty jump shots!" Imagine this activity, if you will. Imagine them lying in their beds, eyes closed but intensely focused. Imagine the involuntary twitches of their leg and shoulder muscles, as they see the ball sailing from their hands to the rim. Imagine them smiling in response to a successful shot, grimacing as one falls to the side. Imagine the intensity of their own imagined experience. You will not be surprised to learn that these players actually improved as a result of this strange exercise.

NLP

Experiences such as these have attracted the attention of psychologists and others interested in developing a theory of imagination. Perhaps the most systematic attempt to describe this phenomenon and to harness it for human good is found in the work of Richard Bandler and John Grinder, the founders of a process known as "Neuro-Linguistic Programming."[1]

Their approach starts from a very simple but striking insight. I have previously said that our images are rooted in past experience. But in truth, those past experiences no longer exist. The only thing that exists now is the image. Hence, in a strange sort of way the image is influencing the experience, rather than experience influencing the image.

Bandler and Grinder also understand the human mind, the home of these images, as being a sort of computer. Indeed, Bandler came to this process not as a psychologist but as a scientist focusing on information technology. But in their judgment the computer-brain is a different sort of computer, one that operates with images rather than with the bits of information that a "computer machine" does. This, of course, is the very same claim that Damasio made.

Put all this together and a conclusion presents itself. We can change our experiences by changing our images. And changing the images is, in a certain sense, a process of reprogramming the brain. Hence the name for their approach—Neuro-Linguistic Programming—reprogramming the language of the brain, which is a language of images.

Bandler and Grinder offer an interesting example of this process.

> Think of a past experience that was very pleasant—perhaps one that you haven't thought about in a long time. Pause for a moment to go back to that memory, and be sure that you see what you saw at the time that pleasant event happened. You can close your eyes if that makes it easier to do. . . . As you look at that pleasant memory, I want you to change the brightness of that image, and notice how your feelings change in response. . . . There are always exceptions, but for most of you, when you make the picture brighter, your feelings will become stronger. Increasing the brightness usually increases the intensity of the feelings, and decreasing brightness usually decreases the intensity of the feelings.[2]

So Bandler and Grinder propose modifying the way in which past experiences affect us in the present by changing the images that survive in our brain. How do they suggest doing this? Two of the techniques they describe, out of many, seem particularly exemplary. Describing them will not only help us to understand NLP; it will also help us clarify the insights that will assist our project of moral formation.

Two Techniques

The first approach makes use of the ways in which we either *associate* or *dissociate* from particular images in our mind. It is curious how many people, at least in their moments of insecurity, will have different ways of imagining past good experiences and bad ones. When they recall bad experiences, they will tend to view them through their own eyes, just as they experienced them when the events originally took place. But when people recall good experiences, they will tend to view them from some other point of view, through the eyes of a bystander or from up above the scene or some such thing. That is, in a subtle but powerful way they will distance themselves from, even disown, the positive experience while taking full ownership for the negative one.

You can imagine the different effects these two points of view have on the abiding feelings stimulated by the image of the past experience. The negative experience is felt very intensely, whereas the positive experience has much less related effect. Not surprisingly, Bandler and Grinder propose reversing this tendency.

This example is best understood in terms of past negative experiences, which, you'll recall, really only exist today in present negative images. Practitioners of NLP would invite the participant to bring to mind the image of the past negative experience. Then, in imagination, they would lead the participant to view that scene from any point of view other than their own. That is, they would encourage the participant to dissociate from that past experience. Doing this produces an almost immediate reduction in the negative feelings associated with the image. Conversely, one can encourage oneself to picture positive images through one's own imaginary eyes, associating with them as deeply as possible. Doing this sort of thing repeatedly, as a sort of exercise, can lead to a deepening of positive feeling and reduction of negative feeling.

A second technique proposed in their writings is called "reframing." This process starts from a simple premise: that the human mind-body unit really desires its own happiness. Consequently, anything that happens within the person is an *attempt* to achieve happiness. If we view this interior happening as a sort of "contribution by some power within," then the contribution must be understood as an utterly sincere and completely genuine attempt to be helpful in this quest for personal happiness. It may not be a skillful or effective contribution, but it is sincere. Even negative feelings, inner attitudes, or inclinations that appear to be profoundly destructive, are nonetheless genuine attempts to be helpful to the self. But if this is true, then any effort to overrule these contributions must avoid condemning them completely. At least the *intent* of the contributions must be honored. Even better, the goal of any personal intervention should be to help this "inner contributor" to find better ways of achieving the good that is actually being sought.

All this will be clearer through an example. People who have difficulty controlling their weight will report a wide range of very powerful feelings. At one moment there will be a tremendous drive to eat. Later there will be an overwhelming sense of guilt and shame at having failed in the attempt to diet. Matters can even become worse when, upon reflection, such people become angry or depressed over the negative feelings already described. It literally is a vicious and unending circle.

Bandler and Grinder would propose another perspective. They would invite us to presume that all of these feelings, from the urge to eat to the surges of recrimination, represent sincere attempts on the part of the mind-body unit to do something good. So rather than criticizing these feelings or being angry about them, they suggest acknowledging them all as friends and helping them become more effective in doing the good that they are trying to do. Take, for example, the sense of guilt and revulsion that comes after having overeaten. They would suggest "befriending" that feeling. What is the feeling trying to accomplish? What good is it attempting to do? Then they would suggest that the participant, in imagination, *negotiate* with the feeling. Affirm the good that it is trying to do; then point out that in some ways it is failing to achieve its own most worthy goal. Ask that feeling if it is willing to try another way to achieve its goal, perhaps through understanding and encouragement. Finally, listen in the expectation that one will actually hear (feel?) a response of affirmation, a commitment to inner collaboration.

This process Bandler and Grinder call reframing. The very process itself involves, as you can see, an extended imaginative activity, which has, as its purpose, the reframing of existing imaginative images within the person.

It is intriguing the way this process can in fact change people and liberate them for more productive behaviors in the future.

Another Example

These comments do not attempt to summarize the theory or the techniques of Neuro-Linguistic Programming. They are merely a few examples. For our purposes, the examples are sufficient if they highlight a simple point. It is true, on the one hand, that the images of imagination are expressive of past experiences, but it is also true that imagination itself is an alternative venue for experience. Indeed, the "experience" that takes place in imagination is at least as powerful as the experiences that happen in the "real world."

In recent years this point has been appreciated and exploited by a wide variety of persons, most of a more practical than theoretical bent. For example, I was introduced to many of these ideas through the intriguing book *The Inner Game of Tennis,* by W. Timothy Gallwey.[3] I read this book not out of any theological interest; I simply wanted to improve my game of tennis! But the insights I discovered there had much broader implications. Gallwey does not acknowledge dependence on Bandler and Grinder, and I do not know if there is a direct connection between them. But the approach is similar.

Like Bandler and Grinder, Gallwey understands the human mind as a sort of computer, often incorrectly programmed and in need of revised programming. He also understands it as a computer that works through images rather than through ideas. Working out from this conception, Gallwey suggests that within each one of us there are "two selves." In terms of the game of tennis, he understands "Self 2" as making the strokes and playing the game. Meanwhile, "Self 1" provides a running commentary on how things are going.

Gallwey then declares:

> within each player the kind of relationship that exists between Self 1 and Self 2 is the prime factor in determining one's ability to translate his [*sic*] knowledge of technique into effective action. In other words, the key to better tennis—or better anything—lies in improving the relationship between the conscious teller, Self 1, and the unconscious automatic doer, Self 2.[4]

Gallwey claims that a lot of the difficulty in tennis, or in many of the activities of life, is a dominating Self 1, screaming instructions and then bitterly complaining when mistakes are made. All of this inner noise, paradoxically, has the effect of preventing Self 2 from simply doing what it wants to do. He declares that

> getting it together mentally in tennis involves the learning of several internal skills: 1) learning to program your computer Self 2 with images rather than instructing yourself with words; 2) learning to "trust thyself" (Self 2) to do what you (Self 1) ask of it. This means letting Self 2 hit the ball; and 3) learning to see "nonjudgmentally"—that is, to see what is happening rather than merely noticing how well or how badly it is happening. This overcomes "trying too hard."[5]

You will notice that Gallwey described the process as a matter of programming images. Later he reinforces this notion in language that is reminiscent of Neuro-Linguistic Programming.

> What is the native language of Self 2? Certainly not words! Words are not learned by Self 2 until several years after birth. No, the native tongue of Self 2 is imagery: sensory images. Movements are learned through visual and feeling images. So the three methods of programming I will discuss all involve communicating goal-oriented messages to Self 2 by images and "feelmages."[6]

Gallwey proceeds to develop these ideas in a popular and intriguing manner that in its details need not detain us. I have no doubt that there are many other popular presentations that would be similar to his. The point that we want to embrace is the centrality of image, the fact that imagination is the alternative venue for experience.

And the reason we want to embrace this conclusion is, of course, because we have every reason to suspect that it will apply in the world of moral living as well as in the world of playing tennis. In this world too, if it is true that moral sensibilities are rooted in experience, it is also true that this experience takes place in two locations: both "out there" and "in here."[7] But if this is really true, then efforts to change people's moral sensibilities can proceed effectively through interventions in either venue of experience. And if that is true, then a most powerful strategy opens for us. We can help teenagers to become sensitive to the needs of the poor, for example, by taking them to a soup kitchen. But we can also help this sensitivity to develop through imaginative exercises stimulating experiences in the "inner world."

Ignatian Contemplation

In some ways, it seems that there is a contemporary rediscovery of this truth. But it is, for all that, merely a rediscovery. The insight into the centrality of imagination has been with us for centuries. Nowhere is this more obvious than in the method of prayer developed by Ignatius of Loyola. Indeed, St. Ignatius is famous in the history of spirituality precisely because of the highly psychological nature of the prayer forms he encouraged.

Teachers of Ignatian spirituality refer to these prayer forms as "contemplation." Interestingly, this term is also used by teachers of prayer in the Carmelite tradition, although the prayer being encouraged is almost exactly opposite in approach to that of Ignatius. In Carmelite contemplation, the goal is to empty the mind of images in order to be quietly present before God, to be centered in silence. In Ignatian spirituality, on the contrary, contemplation is the intentional effort to mobilize imagination in the service of spiritual growth.

The teacher of Ignatian contemplation will invite one to take a passage from scripture, perhaps the story of Jesus meeting Zacchaeus on the road. The spiritual pilgrim is invited to reread that passage. Then she or he is invited to put the Bible aside, to close the eyes and to imagine the scene in as much detail as possible, in "technicolor" if possible. Then, once the scene is etched in the mind's eye, the pilgrim is encouraged to let go, to relax and to allow the scene to unfold in whatever way it will. It is amazing what can happen.

Using this very scene, I can provide an example. A woman once told me the story of her meditation or contemplation on that scene. She was participating in a day of prayer. She had arrived at the retreat house quite harried, having run out of the house with many morning chores left undone. As instructed by the spiritual guide for the day, she read the story of Zacchaeus. Then she quieted herself and imagined the scene of Jesus walking down the road. She imagined herself at the edge of the crowd. She could see Zacchaeus up in the tree. Following the guidelines for this form of prayer, she tried to relax and simply allow the scene to unfold. But it felt uncomfortable and awkward. It did not feel "natural." She felt like she was controlling the contemplation in an unhelpful way. Increasingly, she tried to relax and let go. Suddenly she succeeded; and in that moment her mind's eye found herself not at the edge of the crowd, but up in the tree. This was not what she had planned to do! This was not where she wanted to be. But in faith she allowed the contemplation to proceed.

Jesus came down the road, looked up, and declared: "Eloise, today I am coming to your house." She allowed the contemplation to go on. She was walking down the road with Jesus. And as they walked, she discussed with him many of the issues of her life, her concerns for her children, the complications of her relationship with her husband, and so on. Suddenly, in her mind's eye, they were no longer on a dusty Palestine road. They were on the street of her home. They arrived in front of her house. Without intending to, she heard herself ask Jesus to wait just a moment; she had left the house a great mess, and she wished to tidy up for him. She ran inside, in imagination, and quickly put away the breakfast dishes, made the bed, and stacked the newspapers. And then she returned to the door to invite Jesus in. But he was gone!

This woman told me that she sat quietly in that chapel, in the place of prayer, and began to weep. This contemplation had not gone as she thought it would. In some profound sense it had simply "happened." But she realized, and realized in a profoundly felt way, that her priorities in life were askew. She had been so concerned about images and appearances that she had forgotten what was truly important. Whether it was in her relationship with God, or her efforts with her husband and children, she had been focusing on appearance rather than on substance. The woman reported to me that this time of prayer marked a profound change in her life.

The proponents of Ignatian spirituality believe that the imagination is a privileged pathway through which God can touch our hearts and minds and transform our lives. It is, in that sense, a method of spirituality shaped by and aware of the psychological age.

Other stories, easily as powerful as Eloise's, have been recounted to me. There was the priest who recounted his contemplation of the scene of the transfiguration, in which Jesus walked up the hillside with Peter, James, and John. In imagination the priest stood at the bottom watching them go up the hill. But they got to the top and then nothing happened. Finally Jesus turned, looked down the hill and said, "Fred, we're waiting for you!" The priest reported that this was the moment at which he realized that, even in his apparent ordinariness, he was called to a life of deep prayer.

And there was a layman who spoke of a time when he was considering getting psychological counseling. But part of him felt that this initiative would represent a lack of faith, that he should simply count on God to heal his pain. He was invited, by a spiritual director who was in no way aware of this particular issue in his life, to contemplate the scene of the Good Shepherd. Suddenly, in imagination, he experienced himself as the sheep lying on the shoulders of the shepherd, around his neck. The man reported that he felt very foolish, even to hold such an image in the privacy of his imagination. But in accord with this method of prayer, he let it happen. And, somewhat to his surprise, he found himself whispering in the ear of the Good Shepherd, and talking about his dilemma regarding seeking counseling. He explained to Jesus that he felt he probably should not do it but instead should trust the Good Shepherd to take care of his needs. But then, the man reported, to his utter surprise, in his mind's eye the shepherd turned, looked up into his eyes, the sheep's eyes, and said: "Hey look, I'm not a vet! You need a vet, get a vet! I'm only the Good Shepherd! I can't do everything!" And the man was suddenly liberated, realizing that there was no opposition between trusting in God and making use of human tools.

To appreciate the drama of these examples, one must keep this in mind: they were not planned. They happened in ways that truly and profoundly surprised the persons at prayer. Such is the power of imagination. Such, in the vision of Ignatian spirituality, is the way in which God makes use of imagination to touch our souls.[8]

Conclusion

Our conclusion is simple but profound. Moral sensibilities are a sort of affective knowledge, abiding in feeling more than concept. These sensibilities are shaped by experience, but experience has two venues—out there and in here. We can transform our sensibilities, and we can facilitate the transformation of the sensibilities of others, by interventions in either venue. Indeed, in some ways, interventions in the inner venue of imagination are more powerful, rather than less.[9]

Imagination, then, is a key tool in the making of disciples.[10]

Notes

1. See, e.g., Richard Bandler and John Grinder, *Frogs into Princes* (Moab, Ut.: Real People Press, 1979); Richard Bandler, *Using your Brain—for a Change* (Moab, Ut.: Real People Press, 1985). An excellent recent summary of this perspective is Joseph O'Connor and John Seymour, *Introducing Neuro-Linguistic Programming*, revised edition (San Francisco: Thorsons/HarperCollins, 1995).

2. Bandler, *Using your Brain*, 21.

3. W. Timothy Gallwey, *The Inner Book of Tennis* (New York: Random House, 1974).

4. Ibid., 25.

5. Ibid., 28.

6. Ibid., 56.

7. Many other authors have also explored these ideas. Regarding the roots of imagination in past experience, see Philip Keane's major work, *Christian Ethics and Imagination* (New York: Paulist Press, 1984), especially pp. 86–90. Regarding imagination as experience's second venue, see Daniel Maguire and A. Nicholas Fargnoli, *On Moral Grounds: The Art/Science of Ethics* (New York: Crossroad, 1991), 79–87. For an interesting effort to apply the insights of imagination to the broad range of theological questions, see Kathleen R. Fischer, *The Inner Rainbow* (New York: Paulist, 1983).

8. The "feeling-sensitivity" evident in the Spiritual Exercises of Ignatius is

discussed in detail in Simon Harak, *Virtuous Passions: The Formation of Christian Character* (New York: Paulist Press, 1993), 99–121.

9. A fascinating summary of the relationships of imagination to religious attitudes and behaviors can be found in Andrew Greeley, *The Religious Imagination* (New York: Sadlier, 1981). The date of this publication is significant. Father Greeley was noting, and documenting, the role of the religious imagination well before the theme became common.

10. Also worthy of commendation are the writings of William Lynch, S.J., which explored these themes well before this became common. See especially his *Christ and Apollo* (Notre Dame, Ind.: University of Notre Dame Press, 1975) and *Images of Hope* (New York: Mentor-Omega Book, 1966). The College Theology Society conducted an extensive discussion of Lynch's work in 1996. One observation in particular is amazingly apposite to our discussion. David S. Toolan declares that

> the principle here—that time needs no redeeming, indeed, that the Eternal is to be found in the step-by-step rhythms of time and the "realistic imagination"—is something that Lynch learned, I believe, from the method of prayer in the Spiritual Exercises. This has nothing to do with a slavish, external imitation of Christ. It means using your creative imagination in prayer—inserting yourself into a biblical scene, applying your five senses so that you taste and feel yourself there as an active participant in Christ's archetypal story. If you let your imagination go, the biblical stories do not unfold exactly as they do in the text. No, the story unfolds as the Spirit directs, exactly targeted to where you are in your life.

("Some Biographical Reflections on William F. Lynch's Thought," in *American Catholic Traditions: Resources for Renewal,* ed. Sandra Yocum Mize and William Portier [Maryknoll, N.Y.: Orbis Books, 1997], 133.)

10

The Roles of Story

So there I was, walking down the dusty street at the south end of Calcutta. Mother Teresa was walking at my side. A tiny woman, she barely came to my shoulder. Wrapped in the familiar blue and white sari with the veil over her head, she was telling me about her work with the suffering of the city. It was hot, steamy, the sun glared down upon the brown stucco walls and the packed clay road. I was enthralled by Mother Teresa's description of her work. And I was touched by the way she seemed to be focused entirely on sharing this tale with me.

But suddenly she turned away. She walked away from me, over to the right, to the edge of the road. There, leaning against the wall, was an emaciated old man. He was wrapped in the meanest loin cloth. And he was lying on his side, apparently lacking the energy even to right himself.

I don't think Mother Teresa said a word to him. She stooped down, grasped his shoulders gently, and slid him back to a sitting position. I noticed that she then gently sketched the sign of the cross on his forehead. She wiped his face with the hem of her sari.

Then she turned, walked back to me, and without comment continued the story she had been telling.

AS YOU READ THE PRECEDING PARAGRAPHS, YOU WENT ON AN extraordinary trip. For that brief moment or two, you were not seated in your chair, reading this book. No, you were in Calcutta! Such is the power of story to take us where we have never been, to provide us with experiences we have never before encountered.

The significance of stories for our lives, and for Christian theology, has been discussed by a wide range of authors. Philosophers such as

Alasdair MacIntyre and psychiatrists such as Robert Coles, biblical scholars such as John Dominic Crossan and theologians such as John Shea: all have made important contributions, and I will have occasion to refer to some of their insights before this reflection is over.[1] But the angle I wish to consider is slightly different from theirs, and so our initial question is simple but critical: Why is story so important?

The answer is as straightforward as the story with which we began this chapter. We have already seen that imagination is important because imagination is the second venue of experience. If that is true, then we want to have access to the imaginations of others, to give them the inner experiences that can transform their lives. But how do we gain that access? Through stories! When I tell you a story, I engage the "movie projector of your mind." I touch your imagination. In so doing I do not merely share with you ideas or concepts. No, much more profoundly, I give you an experience. And when you have that experience, it, like all experiences, has the potential to affect your moral sensibilities.

Story, then, is the pipeline to the imaginations of the other. And because it is that, it is also the doorway to expanded life experiences. Having clearly stated this point, however, it will also help us to review some of the insights wherein scholars such as those mentioned above explain how it happens that story touches us so profoundly.

Story's Two Services

Story precipitates experiences in two different ways. First of all, when I tell you a story, whether it is the story of Mother Teresa or the story of my own life, I am to some extent inviting you into the experience that was mine. By mobilizing your imagination, by stimulating within your mind the tendency to actually see the events and be present to them, I am giving you the experiences that I have had. Consequently, the telling of stories involves the sharing of the self in a way that is at least more powerful, and usually more effective, than sharing that is conceptual in style. Thus, stories generate experiences when they manifest the self's experiences to the imagination of the other.

But stories also generate experience within the self in ways that can, indeed, be precipitated by the self. For example, if I, the author of these pages, were to choose to explain to you the moral sensibilities that are central to my life, and not only to name them for you but also to share with you the truth of how they came to be central to me, how would I do that? By sharing my experiences with you, of course. But if I really set out to do that—to share the experiences that have shaped me, I would have to tell you not only of a long list of "real life" experiences that were mine, but also of several "imaginary" experiences. For these "imaginary" experiences have just as surely exercised influence upon my identity.

For example, I would have to tell you about the day when, as a college student, I read John Steinbeck's novel *Of Mice and Men,* about how I devoured the book in a single day, finished it early in the evening, and then, profoundly moved, went to bed with almost no words to anyone. I would have to tell you of the first time I saw the play *Equus* (I have made a point of seeing it several times over the years), of my fascination with the psychiatrist and my sympathy for his question: What is more important, passion or propriety. I would have to tell you of the time I saw the movie *The Deer Hunter* and of how clearly I still see the scene in which a group of Vietnamese play Russian roulette for entertainment, so meaningless are their lives. So powerful was my experience of each of these artistic constructs, that I would have to say that my experience of them was as real as any that happened in the "outside world." The characters who inhabited those works of art are real to me today as they were at the moment of my first encounter. Among my teachers and mentors, then, the models for my life, are George and Lenny, Dr. Dysart, and those nameless citizens of Saigon.

So it is with all of us. Experiences that we have had not in the kingdom of everyday life but in the domain of imagination have nonetheless influenced us as surely as any others. The grace of the artist is her or his ability to so touch our imaginations that we are given an experience that transforms us.

The Theory of Stories

Theologian Stephen Crites is generally credited with the earliest articulation of the significance of story. In a landmark article first published in 1971, Crites explained that all of human experience is essentially narrative in quality.[2] Narrative is not something extra, added to the fabric of life. Rather, narrative is the essential shape that belongs to life precisely because it is life such as we actually live.

And why is that so? Crites suggests that the basis for this truth is very simple: the fact that we all live within time. Human persons are so centrally temporal beings that the fundamental way we understand ourselves is in terms of the temporal flow that is our life's stuff. Our lives, in other words, inevitably have a before and an after, an earlier and a later. There is a temporal quality to time that means that events are unavoidably sequential.

> Past, present, and future cannot be three distinct realities. . . . Only the present exists, but it exists only in these tensed modalities. They are inseparably joined in the present itself. . . . The three modalities are correlative to one another, in every moment of experience.[3]

Consequently, the most "natural" way in which to explain oneself is to recount the events and experiences of one's life. But to present such a recounting is, obviously, to tell a story. "For this tensed unity has already an incipient narrative form."[4] My life, therefore, is more profoundly a story than it is an event or an identity or an idea. The same is true for all persons and, indeed, for all of reality. Because we live in time, reality is intrinsically and centrally narrative.

What is more, says philosopher Alasdair MacIntyre, the story that is our human life is bigger than any one of us. Indeed, we are part of overarching, shared stories. Consequently, one of the functions of telling stories is to show us the part we have been invited to play.

> Man [*sic*] is in his actions and practice, as well as in his fictions, essentially a story-telling animal. . . . But the key question for men is not about their own authorship. I can only answer the question "What am I to do?" if I can answer the prior question "Of what story or stories do I find myself a part?" We enter human society, that is, with one or more imputed characters—roles into which we have been drafted—and we have to learn what they are in order to be able to understand how others respond to us and how our responses to them are apt to be construed. . . . Deprive children of stories and you leave them unscripted, anxious stutterers in their actions as in their words.[5]

Educational psychologist Mark Tappan takes this reflection one step further.

> Whenever it is necessary to report "the way it really happened," therefore, the natural impulse is to tell a story, to compose a narrative that recounts the actions and events of interest in some kind of temporal sequence. Such a story, however, does more than outline a series of incidents; it also places those incidents in a particular narrative context, thereby giving meaning to the human experience of temporality and personal action.[6]

Thus, in the process of constructing the stories that we tell one another, perhaps most especially in the process of composing the "true" stories of our lives, we simultaneously recount events and endow those events with meaning.

Perhaps that is another reason why stories are a powerful influence on the listener. For the imaginative experience that occurs within the listener is, in some paradoxical way, even more real than the experience encountered in the outer world, since it comes already equipped with meaning and intelligibility. As surely as the author had to understand some meaning in the recounted events, so surely did that meaning get communicated. I am not saying that the storyteller allows the narration to degenerate into moralizing, in which the "lesson" is explicitly stated. Rather, in accord with Tappan's insight, I am saying that the very construction of narratives inevitably conveys a certain sense of meaning, if for no other reason, at least because the points almost arbitrarily selected for beginning and end inevitably precipitate some meaning or other. And in a manner far more sophisticated than this "explicit meaning-making," the genius of a wonderful storyteller is precisely the way in which the concreteness of a narrative can communicate meaning not as a secondary addition but as the inner glow of the story itself.[7]

The Need for Stories

You will not be surprised to note that, if stories have the particular virtue of incorporating meaning into "raw experience," stories will tend to arise particularly where we are most in need of the discovery of meaning. Paradoxically, where meaning is least clear in the immediacy of lived experience, there the need for stories is greatest. This point is made powerfully by theologian John Shea. Shea suggests that, in the course of our everyday lives, we inevitably encounter mystery, those elements of our experience which stymie our quest for meaning. Shea suggests five sorts of experiences that cause us this distress.[8]

First there is the experience of contingency, of utter unpredictability. I once avoided an automobile accident when, by pure happenstance, I looked farther to the right than is my usual custom and saw a truck coming around a blind curve. My moralizing self was inclined to chastise me and exhort me to be more careful. But I had a much deeper experience than guilt; I had the experience of life being fundamentally out of my control! No matter how carefully one drives, there are those moments of "luck," whether the vehicle in question be an automobile or one's whole life. What would have happened if I had looked to the left instead of to the right? I will never know. The experience prompted in me a prayer of gratitude. I suppose the very enactment of that prayer represented my expression of meaning in that setting. But the experience was one of contingency.

Although contingency is, in Shea's view, the most common path into the heart of mystery, it is not the only one. Shea also claims that humans experience mystery in moments of interpersonal communion. Here the experience is more one of wonder than of distress, but the central sense that what is going on is beyond the self's control is similar. Another experience that Shea lists is the sad experience of collapse or catastrophe. When things go very badly in our lives, whether in personal failure, in sickness and death, or in betrayal, the sense of mystery is unavoidable. Yet again Shea also takes note of moral ambiguity as an occasion for mystery. In one sense, the meaning of life is comparatively clear when we are confronted by the saintly or the satanic. Overwhelming good and overwhelming evil are not hard to explain. What is far more difficult to explain are those moments of complexity, where events have elements of both good and evil. What shall we make of these experiences?

Finally, and in the way that summarizes the previous four items, Shea names the experience of disenchantment as an occasion of mystery. There are moments in every life when we are overcome by fatigue, by a sense of the hopelessness of it all. The experience is not precisely one of despair; it is rather an experience of dryness, of unimportance, of futility. In such moments one cannot help but ask, in the words of the song, "What's it all about, Alfie?"

In all these moments, then, we are challenged to discover meaning. And how do we do that? We do it, says John Shea, by constructing stories. Often enough the stories are the candid recounting of the events, but because stories fold events into meaning, the result is an assertion of meaning that goes beyond the experience itself.

The Sorts of Stories

These ideas are further developed by theologian Terrence Tilley. As Tilley assesses the scene, it strikes him that human persons generate three distinctively different types of stories. He suggests that it is important to be aware of the different sorts, in order to appreciate the varied power of stories.[9]

First of all, human persons compose "actions." Actions may be positive and upbeat or negative and tragic. They may be happy or sad. They may be exciting or thoughtful. But they have in common the fact that they are set "within the world" as we know it. They accept the world of our lives and the basic vision out of which we already operate. The function of actions is, then, to show us how things go in the world as we know it, to shed light on these worldly patterns and to celebrate them.

In Tilley's judgment, most of the stories that we compose are, in fact, actions. But not all. Tilley suggests that we also compose stories that should be known as "parables." Parables do not accept the world as we now know it. Indeed, the function of parables is to upset the world as we know it. The parables of Jesus are well-known examples of this genre. Each of those stories takes our world and then describes things happening that are quite "wrong" to the world as we know it. In the parables of Jesus what we think is justice is not justice at all. What we usually call success is not really success. The way we expect to be treated, the way that seems "right," is not right at all. And what we think should be the resolution of specific cases is not. But Jesus is not the only writer of parables; the form is larger than him. In all cases, however, the common characteristic of parables is this disruption of our accepted understanding of life.

For that reason parables disturb us. They intrigue, but at the same time they annoy us. So true is this that we often try to defuse parables by explaining them from within our world view. Indeed, this takes place even within scripture, when some of the parables of Jesus are given immediate interpretations. For example, in the Gospel of Matthew, the parable of the sower whose seed fell in various places (13:1–9) is immediately followed not only by a facile interpretation of the parable (13:18–23) but by an interpolated (and rather self-serving) explanation of the function of parables (13:10–17). Scholars tell us that these interpretations in all likelihood do not go back to Jesus. Rather, they were composed in the early years of the church by Christians who could not stand the discomfort of parables standing glaringly on their own. No doubt we do the same with parables that present themselves to us. It is, after all, most troubling to have one's view of life disputed.

Finally, says Tilley, some of our stories are "myths." These are stories which in their power and in their resonance "create a world." That is, they set up a world of understanding; they tell us what life is all about. The first chapters of the book of Genesis are a myth. That is, they are a story that sets out to define the ultimate meaning and shape of our world. If you accept the pertinence of this story, everything in your life takes on a particular meaning. Within this myth, of course, one can go on and compose a myriad of actions, and the actions will make sense because of the myth one has embraced.

The stories of the Greeks, detailing the exploits of their gods, constitute another myth. Perhaps the myth of the Greeks is not utterly contradictory to that of Genesis, but it is certainly not the same. Nor is the myth utilized by Richard Wagner in his cycle of operas, *The Ring of the Nibelungen.* These four operas follow a cast of characters through a complex and powerful story that describes who we are and why our world is the way it is. Other cultures would present yet other myths.

Myths, then, define the world in which we live. In so doing, according to author Joseph Campbell, they serve four functions.[10] First of all, myths have a religious function. That is, they stimulate in us a sense of awe and reverence. John Shea, as we saw, said that our need for stories arises when we confront mystery in our lives. Myths "jump start" that process by stimulating in us a sense of the mystery of life. They speak to the person who might be so captured by the mundane as to overlook the mysterious, and they force such a person to confront the ultimate mystery of life. Thus, myths lead to the religious experience of awe, humility, and reverence.

Once one has such a feeling, of course, one cannot resist the question Why is it so? Answering this question is myth's second function, which Campbell calls the cosmological. That is, myths function to explain how life is and why it is this way. Of course, the word "explain" is being used in a strange fashion, because at another level myths do not explain anything at all. But they do present an overarching feeling that gives meaning to the world and its mystery.

Human persons do not spend all of their time engaging in storytelling, of course. They live their lives! And one of the concerns of society is that people should live their lives in an orderly and productive manner. Myths, curiously enough, serve that goal as well. Campbell says that myths serve a "moral-social" function. That is, to the extent that myths explain why the world is the way it is, they also confirm the established order. As such, they implicitly direct us to cooperate in that order and not to disrupt it. That is, they call us to responsible citizenship.

This call to sociological participation leads to the fourth function of myths, the psychological. It has often been shown that human beings cannot achieve psychological peace until they have clarified their sociological role. That is, I cannot feel at home with myself until I understand how I am at home with those around me. Thus, to the extent that myths define the world and explain its character, to the extent that myths confirm the established order and show me how to participate in it, to that extent myths also allow me to understand myself and to be at peace with myself. Thus, by giving this meaning and context, myths generate a sense of comfort and identity that is extremely fulfilling to human persons.

To be without a myth is to be at sea. To live in the presence of many myths and to have embraced none is to be profoundly divided. But to have a myth, to understand one's self and one's world in a particular way, is to be liberated. Thus myths are the most powerful, if also perhaps the most rare, of stories.

Storytellers for Today

This line of thought suggests that myths are also dangerous things, and that truth leads to a final comment on the topic of stories in our lives. Throughout history, the role of the storyteller has been a pivotal one. Indeed, because of the powerful role of stories in our lives, the storyteller has often been understood as a religious figure. To embrace a storyteller is to accept the stories, and therefore the worlds, which this person may bring. Thus, only a holy person should dare to be a storyteller.[11]

Our modern era, however, faces a powerful new situation. The mass media have created a situation that we can describe as the "centralization of storytelling." The media create a network of communication in which an unprecedentedly small number of people function as the myth makers and storytellers for the whole culture. How powerful such persons are! One cannot help wondering: Are they sufficiently holy for the task?

More than individuals, of course, the storytellers for our culture are corporate entities. Organizations and associations craft our stories. And what are their criteria? Is it the compelling sense of the truth of their stories? Or is it a whole range of extraneous concerns, not least of which is advertising revenue? Of course the latter is true. Thus, we have a situation in which people are profoundly vulnerable to the world views and perspectives of a limited number of anonymous persons, functionaries whose motives in the crafting of their stories may often be venal and false.

This is a very troubling situation. All the more troubling is it because of a second characteristic of mass media culture. At the very moment when the media facilitate the centralization of storytelling, they also discourage lateral communication among audience members. When people went to a public place to hear a story, whether it was the bonfire at the center of the village or the amphitheater in which the drama was presented, they were in one another's presence while they were also in the presence of the story. Thus, there was always, at least in a subtle way, a network of lateral communication. People whispered to one another. People were sensitive to one another's laughs and cries. People nudged one another in response to particular points.

But when the audience is made up of individuals sitting in isolated living rooms, each facing a television tube, there is no way for them to have this lateral communication. The sense of others' reactions to the story is lost. The result is an escalated dependence on the story that is being presented.[12]

Thus, we live in a unique moment in which, paradoxically, story listeners are simultaneously separated from one another and welded to a highly centralized structure of storytelling. Our myths are constructed from the center, and they are constructed in a context in which there is no feedback or evaluation. This is hardly less than a crisis for our society.

What is to be done? Scholars such as John Staudenmeier, who seek to respond to this crisis, call for a constant process of educating the listener. We must at least become more aware of the pitfalls of our cultural setting, less naive about the forces at work in crafting the stories we receive. We need to become sophisticated about the power the media play in our lives. But perhaps something else can also be done. Perhaps we, especially those of us who stand in positions of leadership, who seek to minister to communities of faith, can use our position to contribute to our storied climate.

For one thing, we can help to recreate lateral communication. By talking about our culture's stories, particularly those presented through anonymous media, we can stimulate conversation among other receivers of these stories, trusting that this conversation can do nothing but help. For another thing, we can embrace the role of storytellers for ourselves. We can tell stories, with simplicity but with concreteness, true stories that reflect our personal experience and our communal heritage. We are not "professional" storytellers, of course, but neither were many of the most influential storytellers of history. So it may not be self-deception to imagine that, just perhaps, we may be able to compete with the corporate stories that are delivered to our doorsteps. By multiplying the stories to which people are exposed, perhaps we can excite the imaginations of those we serve, competing on behalf of truth for their hearts and minds.

Conclusion

Stories have many roles, all of them tremendously powerful. Stories are the means by which I share with you the experiences of my life. Through stories I make contact with your imagination, with the movie projector of your mind. In that way I stimulate within you, in the second venue of experience, the experience that has been mine. Thus I give you my experience so that it can become your own. This enriches you at the same moment as it binds us together.

Stories also give *me* experiences. The stories that I see and hear stimulate within me imaginative experiences that are as real as those of the outer world. I am shaped by those stories. Perhaps no more profoundly am I shaped than by the myths that define my world. But I am also shaped by the parables and the actions that I encounter.

There is nothing more important, then, than the "truth" of our stories. Truth, you will realize, has little to do with factual history. It has everything to do with insight and authenticity. People wonder: Shall I ask about the truth of the story? Of course you should ask. But do not be deceived by the simple answer that focuses on whether "it happened" or not. Rather, seek endlessly for the deeper answer: Is it true to what is? Is it true to reality? Is it true to myself? Is it true to God? And when stories have this truth, then let them be repeated without ceasing.

For only these stories, creations of truth and beauty, can facilitate the making of disciples.

Notes

1. Alasdair MacIntyre, *After Virtue* (Notre Dame, Ind.: University of Notre Dame Press, 1981); Robert Coles, *The Call of Stories* (Boston: Houghton Mifflin Co., 1989); John Dominic Crossan, *The Dark Interval: Towards a Theology of Story* (Niles, Ill.: Argus Communications, 1975); John Shea, *Stories of God* (Chicago: Thomas More Association, 1978).

2. Stephen Crites, "The Narrative Quality of Experience," in *Why Narra-*

tive? ed. Stanley Hauerwas and L. Gregory Jones (Grand Rapids, Mich.: Eerdmans, 1989), 65–88.

3. Ibid., 76–77.

4. Ibid., 77.

5. MacIntyre, *After Virtue,* 201.

6. Mark B. Tappan, "Narrative, Authorship, and the Development of Moral Authority," in *Narrative and Storytelling: Implications for Understanding Moral Development,* ed. Mark B. Tappan and Martin J. Packer, New Directions in Child Development 54 (San Francisco: Jossey-Bass, 1991), 8.

7. Many of these ideas on the importance of story are splendidly explored from a social science perspective by Paul Vitz, "The Use of Stories in Moral Development," *American Psychologist* 45 (June 1990): 709–20. At the same time, this whole vision of narrative is not without its critics. Though I am not finally persuaded by his arguments, significant issues are raised in Daniel Beaumont, "The Modality of Narrative: A Critique of Some Recent Views of Narrative in Theology," *Journal of the American Academy of Religion* 65 (1997): 125–39.

8. Shea, *Stories,* 25–36.

9. Terrence Tilley, *Story Theology* (Collegeville, Minn.: Liturgical Press, 1985), 39–53.

10. According to Tilley, *Story Theology,* 42–44.

11. A wonderful summary of the holy activity of storytelling can be found in William Bausch, *Storytelling: Imagination and Faith* (Mystic, Conn.: Twenty Third Publications, 1984).

12. This issue has been forcefully presented by John Staudenmeier, a historian of culture who teaches at the University of Detroit. Through several lectures heard on different occasions, I have been privileged to learn from Staudenmeier's careful analysis and provocative proposals.

11

The Body's Other Language

I HAVE A FANTASY. IT IS THE END OF THE SECOND VATICAN Council, that momentous event by which the Roman Catholic Church struggled to engage the realities of the modern world and to present the perennial truths of the faith in an appropriate, really responsive way. In pursuit of this objective, the council has engaged in extended reflection and energetic debate. These interactions have led to the construction of a series of historic documents

Many would identify as the central document of Vatican II the Dogmatic Constitution on the Church, *Lumen Gentium*. And with good reason, since this document offered a powerful proclamation of a modified, enriched, renewed vision of the church. What is that vision? Perhaps it is best summarized in the words that entitle the document's second chapter: "The People of God." That is, in the council's view the church is not most fundamentally an institution or a structure. Nor is it a set of hierarchical offices or personages. Rather, it is most basically a community, a group of persons called by Christ to live the faith, to undertake discipleship, to mediate salvation to a needy world, and to serve the Lord by serving one another and all creation.

A wonderful, exciting vision, evidently rooted in scripture, expressive of the deepest, most ancient traditions of the church—and *Lumen Gentium* offers a powerful proclamation of it. But there is a problem. In all truth, very few members of the church have ever read *Lumen Gentium*. Probably very few readers of these words of mine have read the entire document. Indeed, I would be surprised if all the current leaders of the church have read it. So if the bishops of Vatican II actually hoped to transform the self-understanding of Catholics around the world through the document they so carefully crafted, they are liable to be sadly disappointed.

And here is where my fantasy takes over. I imagine the bishops struggling to craft this historic document and, at the end, feeling pride at their accomplishment. They are tired, too, of course; so they are eager to head for home. But then, suddenly, at the last moment, almost as an afterthought, they take one final action. They issue an instruction.

> We know it's a small thing, and we hope you won't mind. But we think it might be a good idea to express this vision of Church as a People of God in our worship. So, would you mind terribly? When you go to Mass on Sunday, could you please, before you receive the Lord in communion, just take a moment to turn to your neighbor and shake hands? Wish peace, say hello. No big thing, just a modest gesture. Could you? Would you? Thanks!

And that instruction has made all the difference. Many of us are old enough to recall when we began enacting this gesture: how *wrong* it felt! Church was a place to be quiet, to focus solely upon God. Church was a place we went to, entered. Church was an organization we belonged to, depended on. Church was where the neighbor was a distraction, something to be ignored. Church was me and God. . . . Or perhaps, me, the priest, and God.

Luckily we were sufficiently loyal members of this church that, even when the instruction felt so wrong, we did as we were told. Perhaps we also asked questions, demanded to understand the reasons for the request. But one way or another, we went ahead and did it. As awkward and inappropriate as it felt, we turned and greeted our neighbors. And little by little, over months or years, the gesture won out! In the face of the body's language, ideology didn't stand a chance! The body's actions dragged our understandings, kicking and screaming, from one vision of church to another.

Thus, by the simple expedient of a modest gesture of peace-wishing, far more than by the lofty words of a document, the bishops of Vatican II reconstructed the theology of church of a worldwide, multicultural, often uneducated, and sometimes unresponsive congregation in the astonishingly brief period of twenty years.

Perhaps I exaggerate matters somewhat. But there is surely a kernel of truth in this reflection. And to the extent that it is true, this fantasy manifests the insight to be explored in this chapter: the power of the language of body.

Enfleshed Spirits

In his intriguing book *A Theology of Presence,* Richard Westley develops an understanding of human persons that sees them (us!) as enfleshed spirits, not as rational animals, as is often asserted. Like all beings that are spiritual, our existential fulfillment is achieved by communion, by that connection with other beings that is achieved through intellect and will, that is, by understanding and love. When we understand other beings, when we achieve genuine insight, then communion occurs, and communion brings a sort of fulfillment to the spirit. When we reach out in love, when we commit ourselves to others in concern and compassion, then communion occurs. And communion brings a sort of fulfillment to the spirit.

But the human person, says Westley, is an *enfleshed* spirit. We are that sort of spirit that can achieve the goals of spirit only through body. We are not temporarily connected to our body, trapped in a sort of Platonic prison until we are released into the realm of pure spirit. No, we are permanently related to matter, so much so that, as Catholic theology proclaims, our final fulfillment will occur not only as a result of "the immortality of the soul" but also and essentially as a result of "the resurrection of the body."

That is why Aquinas can declare that all human knowledge is *cognitio per sensus,* knowledge by way of the senses. That is why the loss of any of our senses—sight, hearing, touch—is a fundamental loss, not just a disability of the body but a hobbling of the spirit. That is why the teacher Annie Sullivan could not bring light to the wonderful spirit of Helen Keller until she could find a sensate door through which to contact that inner realm. The famous scene where she forced Keller's hand under running water while tapping the braille equivalent of "water" is a moving lesson in that truth. And that is why the focusing and purifying of the senses are part of the spiritual discipline of all the great religions.

But if the achievement of our human goal, communion, can occur only through the body, what exactly do we have to work with? Westley responds: "Given what has been said, *we have only two things at our disposal with which to do the work of the spirit....* And what are those two things? Our *words* and *physical presence,* of course."[1] Or, if I may use slightly different terms to say the same thing, we have *word* and *gesture*, and nothing else, with which to do the work of spirit.

In large part, the last two chapters have explored the power of words to serve spirit. And we have discovered that words, especially imaginative words, words combined into images and parables and stories, are powerful indeed. Now we need to look at the body's other language, the language of gesture and the language of gesture's sophisticated child, ritual.

Gesture

The nonverbal language of gesture is not only the body's "other" language; it is also the body's first language. Indeed, the colloquial name for gesture is "body language." So we have body language before the body achieves language. Anyone who has ever held a baby knows that babies communicate long before they have words. So the language of the nonverbal is really primary, even if we do come to our discussion of it at the end. And it is primary not only in the sense of coming first; it is also in some ways more central to human personhood.

Recently, I found myself standing by the curb outside a large airport terminal. A car sitting next to the curb was ready to pull away, but the path was blocked by a double-parked van. A man riding in the car got out and with growing agitation shouted at the van's driver, a woman who was alone except for a small dog. I could not see the woman. I do not know if she was expressing cavalier disregard for the others' wants, although my sense was that, in the tight confines of the moment she was unable to pull forward and afraid to attempt backing up. Finally, the man reared back and kicked the side of the van.

Several of us were shocked into action, shouted at the man, and (apparently) dissuaded him enough that he got back in his car. A moment later the car in front of him drove away, opening a path that allowed his car to depart. With considerable relief we watched the episode come to an end.

I hardly endorse the man's violent gesture. Indeed, its aggressiveness galvanized several of us into action. But later reflection led me to acknowledge its authenticity. The moral problem, if we would speak this way, was not in the kick; it was in the aggression that preceded it. The gesture did nothing more than express with terrifying faithfulness the sentiments of the embodied spirit we were observing. And this taught me several things. First, it showed that efforts to muzzle our genuine views in a sort of "gestural silence" are very likely to fail. The language of the body lurks always near the surface, and it will not easily be denied. Whether the gesture is murderous or contemptuous or domineering, or on the other hand affirming or celebrating or consoling, the body desires to speak. Thus, as a second learning, I saw that we must tend to the spirits of persons (no doubt through new and different gestures) so that the body language these spirits crave is itself more positive. The goal, in other words, is not just that this man should not kick the van; the goal is that he should not harbor such feelings about the woman inside that he *wants* to kick the van. For the language of body is, indeed, the primary language of human persons.

Third, I learned that false language, even if it is in fact possible for human persons, nevertheless exacts a very high price. Even the briefest reflection on the human capacity for language should lead us to declare that persons are somehow "made for truth." At the least, truth telling is easier than lying, since one doesn't have to take care to remember what one said! More deeply, in Westley's language, how can we achieve communion if it is not communion in truth? So, lying in some ways "goes against the grain" of what it means to be human. But we can lie, at least in the short term, even if we shouldn't.

We can lie with our words, speaking falsehood with the intent to deceive those who deserve truth. It is sometimes hard to find the words of deception, but we can do it. Much more difficult, however, is to lie with our bodies. Indeed, polygraph machines work precisely because the body finds it so difficult to lie! If I express false words, my body rebels. And with electrical impulse, with dilation of blood vessels and the blushing that follows, with the tightening of breath and the quickening of pulse, the body testifies to the truth that will not be spoken.

Sadly, though, even the body can lie. Enemies can proffer the handshake that is false. Lovers can masquerade manipulation in gestures of care and commitment. Smiles can hide disdain, nods can camouflage denial. But since gesture is the body's first language, when lying becomes embodied, a very serious calamity has occurred, a deep and disturbing human confusion follows. For when we cannot trust our bodies and the bodies of others, we are literally "all at sea." And that is tragedy indeed.

Finally, and paradoxically, this tragedy of falsehood can occur also when we become so alienated from our bodies that they cannot comfortably provide any expression at all to what is felt within. The effort to make the body's sexual language authentic, for example, is not only a project in self-control for the uncommitted. It is also a project in self-expression for lovers. Ask the long-married to talk about their journey to true "nakedness," for example.[2] The same dynamic is visible also in less intimate gestures. Those raised in repressive environments can feel the bite of envy when they observe the comfortable kisses shared within families from other backgrounds. To receive a spontaneous hug is a thrilling (even if also vaguely discomforting) gift. And there is something quite beautiful about the elderly person so at home with himself or herself, that touch is genuine, comfortable, and free.

Ritual

If the language of body is so important, however, we should not be surprised at human efforts to facilitate it. And where large numbers of persons are involved, this effort involves the constructing of a common vocabulary, a sort of shared body language. That, in the end, is what we mean by ritual.[3]

Consider the many simple domestic rituals that enrich our lives. The birthday cake, aglow with candles, entering the darkened dining room. Stories read before bedtime—not the content of the stories but the body language of the event itself, dressed in pajamas, cuddling on couch or bed. The pantheon of "family feasts." For some reason, it became established years ago in my own family that the time our extended family gathers is not Christmas, as it is with many others, but Thanksgiving. To this day, the married cousins make much more effort to attend that celebration than any other; it is a "ritual" of ours.

Think of school rituals that facilitate the journey to maturity. Opening day receptions, processes of introduction during a course's first class, rituals of matriculation, transition, graduation. At the school where I teach, an outstanding student from each college is chosen annually. The students are honored at a luncheon for the "grown-ups." They are then the guests of honor at the evening dance provided for the collegians. Indeed, the honored students form a receiving line through which all the party-goers are expected to pass: a powerful gesture expressing the importance of scholarly, moral, and social excellence. Many are the undergraduates whose perception of college has been modified by an encounter with this ritual. I am also aware of a Catholic college where, during the annual commencement ceremony, all those graduates who are planning to spend the next year in one or another of the many volunteer movements (Peace Corps and the like) are called forward for a special blessing. The power of the ritual, speaking to graduates and observers alike, is evident.

Think also of more ambiguous rituals. Hazing ceremonies of fraternities surely walk the thin line between bonding activities and sadism, but rituals of this sort have long existed. Some scholars have argued that the practice of insisting that young doctors work twenty-four-hour shifts in the emergency room survives in the face of extensive research showing its harmfulness because it has become a ritual of maturation among medical practitioners, a shared ordeal, a sort of puberty rite for doctors!

And think of religious rituals. Some are regular, recurring rituals such as the ceremony of ordinary Sabbath worship. Others are singular, attending to the religious significance of major human events: birth, entrance into adulthood, the creation of family, death. Some are central to the vision of a formal religious tradition, such as the sacraments. Others are peripheral, though not for all that any less important to their participants. One thinks of novenas, of the Marian celebrations of different ethnic groups, of pilgrimages and the like.[4] But their common characteristic is that they are structured and stylized sets of gestures allowing a large number of people to express, in the body as much as in words, convictions, and feelings that are central to their lives.

Of course, rituals are not always so, and there is something singularly sad about religious rituals that have been emptied of significance for a particular group. For many Catholics, that is exactly what had happened in the years before Vatican II; for some Catholics it is what has now happened as a result of the liturgical renewal. And there is something singularly frightening about religious rituals that have been coopted, even prostituted to other goals. Many clergy talk with genuine anger about weddings in which there seems to be no religious sentiment, just the mounting of a social event. One priest once told me of a parish situation where after funerals he often found communion wafers stuck in the pages of hymnals. Participants seemed to find it socially unacceptable not to receive communion. But somehow, judging themselves unworthy of reception, they felt it was less culpable to secretly dispose of the wafer than to swallow it.

But when rituals are truly expressive of the convictions of the participants and responsive to their needs, they allow for an experience of common humanity, of solidarity in identity and mission, that nothing else can create. They are, in a sense, the dance of the persons we would like to be, the enactment of the sort of world we would like to create. As such, they are empowering. The ritualized gestures in which we participate deepen the sense of identity, empower the sense of mission, so that the dance can, to a growing degree, be danced in the ordinary affairs of one's life.[5]

As we saw in previous chapters, in our discussions of the power of the group to maintain and support particular value priorities, we are all tremendously dependent on the groups to which we belong. What we now realize is that when the group gathers for common worship, it mediates its commonly shared values in several ways, not just one.

First of all, liturgical celebrations support the life of discipleship by the very *fact* of their existence as common worship, by the presence of others who, as an immediate consequence of their very presence, are testifying to their share in the effort to love our neighbors as ourselves. Second, as we now see clearly, liturgical ritual supports the life of discipleship by the body language, the language of ritual gesture, that is commonly enacted when the group comes together. Standing and sitting, making the sign of the cross, bowing at certain words, sharing the procession to communion, and feeding from common plate and cup: all these ritual gestures reinforce and strengthen the values of the group. Third, as an important but still tertiary factor, the words that are spoken, the message shared in sermon, the vision proclaimed in hymn and prayer make their contribution to the power of the ritual.[6]

Conclusion

Rituals do not fulfill all the needs of the human person, even of the person as a gesturing being. They have an undoubted power; indeed, in their very generality they allow human body communication that would otherwise be impossible. But there is a certain formality to rituals that limits their usefulness. They do not allow the spontaneity that generates intimacy, that precipitates the kind of close communication, verbal and otherwise, that is ultimately essential to the communion of enfleshed spirits. Perhaps, then, a certain peak of authentic body language can be found in those rare moments when predetermined ritual and spontaneous and authentic gesture meet. By way of conclusion to this chapter, let me describe such a moment.

On November 14, 1996, Cardinal Joseph Bernardin, the archbishop of Chicago, died after a long illness. The esteem in which he was widely held because of the work of his life was only enhanced by the candor and courage of his final days. As a result, his funeral, held on November 21, was a very special moment.

The progressive nature of his illness meant that local officials had been given time for careful planning, and in all the ceremonies surrounding the cardinal's death this planning was evident. Ceremonies were conducted with both theological soundness and aesthetic taste. At the same time positive feelings for the cardinal led to the attendance of an extraordinarily large delegation of dignitaries, which was complemented by an overflow congregation of local clergy and laity who came out of genuine, deep feeling. The result was liturgical ritual of almost unparalleled power. If ever a ritual served its purpose, allowing personal strangers to join, through languages of both word and gesture, in an act fully meant and deeply felt, it did so in this funeral.

But something more contributed to this funeral. As we have seen, the very formality of ritual leaves it inevitably partial, somehow constricting at the same time as it is liberating. And for a certain period in the early moments of this funeral, that constriction was evident. There was an uncomfortable rigidity, a formalism, that was disappointing. Perhaps it was the collective reaction of the congregation to the presence of civic and religious notables; perhaps the obvious presence of the TV cameras. In any case, the mood was stiff.

But then came the homily. The preacher, at Cardinal Bernardin's request, was Father Kenneth Velo. Father Velo had been the cardinal's secretary and assistant and, as is often customary in this role, he had lived at the cardinal's residence. The result, however, was that he had become the cardinal's friend, and it was that identity that led to his being selected preacher.

Father Velo spoke eloquently. But because he spoke as a friend, he felt free to speak also with humor, commenting on Cardinal Bernardin's foibles. Laughter began, cutting the formality of the moment with a gentle knife of warmth. In response to a particularly endearing comment, applause erupted, hesitant at first and then firm. An energy began to pulse through this huge, diverse but bonded congregation. Twice more in the course of the homily, the congregation expressed its spontaneity in applause.

And then came the final, touching words: "Cardinal, Eminence. You're home! You're home!" Father Velo stepped away from the pulpit. There was a moment of silence, a hushed, almost breathless sharing of truth. And then the applause again. Was it applause for Father Velo? Perhaps, at least at first; although even in those first seconds it felt more like applause in the joy of the shared moment of love and faith.

But in any case, not for long. Suddenly, members of the congregation began rising to their feet. Soon the entire congregation arose. The applause seemed to congeal and then grow. Now it was, quite evidently and overwhelmingly, a standing ovation for—perhaps even to—Cardinal Joseph Bernardin. Nothing more, and nothing less.

And in that moment the intimate power of spontaneous gesture joined to the public power of ritual to make a statement that cannot be translated, and that will never be forgotten by those who experienced it. No words were necessary because no words were possible. This statement was in a deeper language of the human person. It was the language of the body, the first and ultimate language of the enfleshed spirit. And it said something—probably said many things—that nourished and enlivened, touched and transformed, consoled and renewed, embraced and encouraged all those who were honored by the experience.

Of such statements are disciples finally made.

Transition

We come now to the end of part 3 of our project. Earlier we saw that peoples' value priorities, affectively felt, are shaped by experience. We noted that experience happens in groups, that we are consequently influenced in profound and lasting ways by the groups to which we belong, by the relationships that nourish and sustain us, by the mentors and models that show us the way.

But there is another angle in all this, we now see. In part 3 we have learned that human experience presents itself in two venues, not just one. And in some ways the second venue is yet more powerful than the first. It is in the world of imagination that our values are most deeply shaped and reshaped. Because imagination makes contact with the movie projector of the mind, it precipitates experiences that touch and transform us. Through imagination I make you the gift of my "real life" experiences, as I recount them to you, and through imagination I make myself the gift of experiences I might never have in real life, as I enter the world of fiction, of narrative artfully crafted to illuminate deeper truths of life.

In all this, then, it becomes clear that story cuts a pathway for imagination. But it is only one pathway of two. For human persons speak two languages, those of word and gesture. So, finally, we came to consider the language of gesture, of spontaneous body movement and of formalized rituals both secular and religious. And we discovered the

incomparable ability of the body's other language to carry imagination, to precipitate experiences in the second venue, and thus to energize, support, and guide the values out of which we daily live.

With these thoughts we come to the end of our exploration. The
questions confronted us: How do people come to embrace the values
out of which they live? And how are these values modified? Our journey into the scholarship of theology and philosophy, psychology and
sociology has provided answers to these questions.

But our project is not really complete. For we had a deeper question,
a question that stood just beyond these theoretical queries: What
might this mean for the making of disciples? After all, our interest was
not speculative; we wanted to make a difference. So now the time has
come to seek the "payoff" for our efforts. In part 4 I will attempt to
apply the insights of these scholarly investigations to the ministerial
project. I will guide our attention to three topics: religious education,
liturgical worship, and parochial life. In each case, I will seek to mine
these insights, bringing to the surface their implications for concrete
action. I will share examples of success that I have found, and I will propose ideas for further consideration.

In doing this, then, I will invite us finally to embrace the central role
of the minister, the making of disciples.

Notes

1. Richard Westley, *A Theology of Presence* (Mystic, Conn.: Twenty Third
Publications, 1988), 14 (emphasis in original).

2. I have used this vision of moral sexuality as "true gesture," with moral
challenges both of control and transparency, in *The People's Catechism*, ed. Ray-
mond Lucker, Patrick Brennan, and Michael Leach (New York: Crossroad,
1995), 226–27.

3. The role of ritual and the implications of these ideas for Christian
liturgy are given powerful expression by Tom E. Driver, *The Magic of Ritual*
(San Francisco: HarperCollins, 1991).

4. See Patrick L. Malloy, "The Re-Emergence of Popular Religion Among
Non-Hispanic American Catholics," *Worship*, forthcoming.

5. The power of liturgical ritual to empower moral conversion is beautifully described by Harmon L. Smith, *Where Two or Three Are Gathered* (Cleve-
land: Pilgrim Press, 1995).

6. An interesting effort to connect liturgy and morality can be found in
Patricia Ann Lamoureux, "Liturgy of the Hours and the Moral Life," *New Theology Review* 10 (1997): 40–57. Still, it is significant that her primary focus is
the power of the *words* to effect moral formation. Our focus here is the power
of the *gesture* to do the same.

PART 4

STRATEGIES FOR

PASTORAL MINISTRY

12

Inviting Discipleship

IN THIS FINAL PART OF THE BOOK I WANT TO INDICATE SOME of the implications of our research for the project of "making disciples." There is no way to explore all the implications, but by the same token, many of them have really become obvious as I developed the insights of the previous chapters. So the goal here will simply be to tease out a few particularly helpful points. And in doing so, I will look at three key activities of the faith community, as it pursues its vocation to make disciples: religious education, liturgical worship, and parish life.[1]

What Is Religious Education?

I should begin with a few words defining what I mean by religious education, for the term is understood in quite diverse ways. For example, some people seem to see the purpose of religious education as the passing on of "the faith," by which they understand an objective and essentially cognitive set of truths. Others see it as the inculcation of a set of behavioral norms, such that education's consumers will behave in an upright, even conventional manner. Many a parent, for example, sends the children to Catholic school for "ethical training." Yet others see it as nothing more than the providing of insights into religion, with little or no expectation of personal commitment.

My view is different. I take as my starting point those words of Jesus that have shaped this book: "Go . . . and make disciples of all nations" (Matt. 28:18–19). This is the command Jesus imposes on all his followers. So the making of disciples is the whole purpose of the church. Religious education is not identical with that task; it only makes a contribution to it. And what sort of contribution? An educational one, of course.

I realize that this doesn't remove all the ambiguity, since education is itself subject to many interpretations. But rather than belabor that discussion, which in the end doesn't make all that much difference, let me simply settle for a synthesizing definition.

For me, religious education is a set of activities that systematically exposes people to the convictions of the Christian community in such a manner that they are invited to—even encouraged to—embrace the life of discipleship. And religious educators are those persons who, while entering into the ministerial life of the church and into the church's overarching project of making disciples, see themselves also as members of an educational guild, root their activities in the insights of educational experts, and find support in the presence of others who similarly define themselves.

What is Discipleship?

But defining religious education doesn't exhaust these preliminary remarks. It will also prove helpful if I say a few words to clarify further what I mean by "discipleship." I believe this theme can be summarized in five terms.

First, discipleship is a relationship, specifically a relationship with God and with God's son, Jesus, such that one defines oneself as a "follower." Second, discipleship involves understanding, since no one lives a relationship with the unknown. Whether my relationship is to a person or to a cause, the object of my loving commitment must first of all be known. Third, discipleship involves just this commitment, a cleaving to the object of my love such that maintaining the relationship becomes a personal, ongoing priority. Fourth, discipleship involves enacted fidelity, behavior in which I act in a manner consonant with my commitment, expressive of this love that is my priority. And fifth, inasmuch as human persons are essentially social, discipleship involves affiliation with others similarly committed, such that support is given and received, wisdom offered and accepted.

Discipleship, then, is relationship, understanding, commitment, behavior, and affiliation. And if this is so, it is to this that religious education invites. But how is that done? The remainder of this chapter represents some answers to that question. I want to mine the insights of this book's exploration, allowing them to influence the practice of religious education, and in so doing, I will explore seven themes.

Identity

Samuel Oliner's fascinating research into the motivations of Christians who befriended Jews in the Nazi era highlights a simple, central fact: people live out of abiding identities. The individual choices that comprise a life are not unconnected moments of freedom. Rather, they are a certain kind of mountain peak, so to speak, in a mountain range of selfhood. When moments of special choice arrive, people tend to make their decisions almost automatically. For in a certain sense the really important decision has long since been made.

So it is clear that religious education is an enterprise in the shaping of personal identity. It is about formation, not information. Indeed, whatever information is shared in religious education (and it most certainly has a place) is shared precisely because it can serve the process of identity formation.

This is a very helpful point. Catechetical leaders tell me that people are often very hesitant to serve as teachers, and the reason they give is that they don't have sufficient knowledge of the faith. By this they mean that they feel deficient in theological literacy. How freeing it is to assure these teachers that they are not expected to have all the answers.

I experienced this liberation myself, years ago. I have often given workshops in moral theology; and in the early years of doing so, I often felt considerable tension from the expectation that I should be able to answer all questions. Indeed, to escape the tension I once briefly considered trying to limit the kinds of questions I would permit. But then, luckily, gracefully, I saw another path. And I began the practice of starting my workshops with O'Connell's Rule: "You reserve the right to ask any question you like, and I reserve the right to say I don't know!" A similarly liberating arrangement should be offered to every catechist. For as one commentator put it, in the first instance you are not teaching the faith, you are teaching the children.

Of course, this focus upon formation, rather than information, is not entirely liberating. For it leaves before us the equally troubling question: How does formation take place? Again, our research helps answer that question, returning repeatedly to the central role of personal relationship. So the religious educator is in the business of cultivating relationships—indeed, a wide variety of relationships. Let's explore several in turn.

Relationships

First, there is the relationship with the catechist herself or himself. I was deeply inspired one time, when I came upon a parish where the leaders took the importance of relationship so seriously that they designed their entire high school program around it. Previously, the parish had followed the common practice of holding the classes in the homes of the teachers. But like many parishes they had also designated the various teacher-couples as "freshman parents," "sophomore parents," etc., so that the students moved from home to home with each passing year. Eventually, however, the administrators really thought about this practice and noticed the contradiction hiding within it. They realized that, for all their talk of relationship, the curricular arrangement symbolically suggested a content-oriented program, not a person-oriented one. (In noting this they were, of course, learning our lesson about the importance of body language.) "Isn't it easier," they decided, "for the catechists to learn new material than for the students to enter a new relationship?" Having answered that question, they redesigned the program.

This is how it worked. The administrators would approach a married couple, active members of the parish. They would invite the couple to contribute to religious education. "We know that many factors may modify your availability," they would say. "But presuming things don't change, would you make a four-year commitment to our program? We will give you a group of freshmen, and we will ask you to stay with them until they graduate. We will help you master the new textual materials each year; you will not have to worry about that. What we will ask of you is that you try to remain a part of these young people's lives through these important years."

This arrangement created continuity in the classroom, of course, but it did so much more. In one case, the teens baby-sat the couple's children. In another, they helped out when the couple moved to a new house. One couple took the teens on a summer outing to the woods.

When the brother of one of the participants was killed in an automobile accident, another couple brought the group together to grieve and to provide support. In many cases the teens practically became part of the couple's family. And, as I understand it, many of them remain in contact to this day.

In a word, the program allowed relationships to develop, and through those relationships it powerfully invited the young people into a life identity and life-style of discipleship.[2]

What is going on in these relationships is, of course, the process of modeling, for values are appropriated through modeling, through life's constant process of observation and imitation. But because this is true, well-thought-out religious education programs multiply relational opportunities. Activities are developed that take the participants beyond their immediate setting, connecting them to other impressive people who can provide them with additional example and insight. Inspiring individuals are brought into the classroom, not to teach but simply to share. And participants are sent out to meet, to observe, to interview, to experience.

All this can be humbling, of course, as the teacher realizes that she or he is not the only influence in the lives of the participants. It takes maturity to accept that one is not so much the teacher as simply the organizer of learning and growing experiences, an asceticism that is an essential part of religious education (and, indeed, of all ministry).

A leader in a religious congregation of women once told me of a plan to bring together novices from several different groups for a summer experience. The thought was that, with the reduced number of women entering religious life, this wider sharing would give a heightened sense of support. Alas, the program was applauded by *almost* everyone. The sole exception: the novice supervisors of the individual groups. Unlike everyone else, they were suspicious of this program, presenting objections, pointing out dangers. And it eventually became clear that their suspicion was largely a function of something else: their fear of a loss of influence!

My conversation partner told me that the program was held in spite of these objections and that it was a great success. What is more, she added, her community has since decided that no one will do formation work on a full-time basis. "They start to need it too much," she told me. Instead, the sisters assigned to this work continue also their other work, teaching perhaps or working in a hospital, and they provide formational leadership "on the side," as a generous and hopefully less need-driven activity.

Groups

Religious education is focused on relationships then. But not just relationships between participants and leaders. The relationships within the group are pivotal too, since, as we have seen, identity is shaped by group. The research of Norma Haan, among others, has made it perfectly clear: we are a function of our groups. We live up to—or down to— the standards of the groups to which we belong. And if our values diverge greatly from those of our groups, we inevitably move along.

When I was in graduate school, I became involved in the university's campus ministry program. In particular, I provided support to a group of undergraduates who were themselves serving as peer ministers within the college. Midway through the year a crisis developed. Two of the group's members began dating and became increasingly involved with each other. Eventually circumstances made it clear that they were sleeping with each other.

A wide range of complex struggles arose. I myself struggled, seeking to define my role. Should I be the spokesman for moral rightness? Eventually I decided that a more helpful role would be for me to support the group's wrestling with the issues, and the group did indeed struggle. They not only had ethical objections to the couple's behavior; they also experienced it as a betrayal. The couple had, they felt, violated the implicit covenant of the group to model the highest Christian values to the school. At the same time, they were divided about what to do. They could argue that the way of Jesus demanded a certain standard of sexual behavior, but they also felt strongly that the way of Jesus was a way of compassion and understanding. These two values struck them as being in excruciating conflict.

Finally, the group attempted to resolve the matter through dialogue with the young man and woman who were the center of the controversy. This precipitated a third experience of struggle. For, to put it in words that only came to me years later, the group discussion made it clear to the couple that, in their fixation on each other, they no longer held dear the values for which the group stood. In Rokeach's terms, their priorities had shifted. They also resented the group's intrusion, an expression both of how important this relationship was to them and of the power of American individualism. In any case, it eventually became clear to the couple that no resolution but one was possible: the two of them must withdraw from the group.

There was much sadness at the end of this experience. But also much wisdom, I believe. I certainly learned from it. I believe the members of the group also learned a great deal, appreciating more deeply than before the cost of values—and the importance of groups. And it is this lesson that shapes the strategies of successful religious education programs, where much energy is spent on group development. The group is provided constant opportunities to interact, to reinforce, to support, and to challenge.

Communication

It is obvious that what is going on in these groups is communication, but a few expanded observations may help here. First of all, it is certainly true that religious education involves a good bit of instructional conversation. But we should remind ourselves that the mode of this conversation is not one of bald command. Its objective is not to tell the participants what to believe or how to behave. Rather, as an example of the activity of induction, the communication should combine expectation and explanation. It should speak boldly about the way of life that is expected of members of this group. But when the participants inevitably ask why, a candid answer should be forthcoming. Leaders should speak from the heart about why these values are important to them, why the group espouses this particular way of life.

Second, the conversation should be experience-based. The focus should not be: "This is what the textbook (or the magisterium or the Bible) says." Rather it should be: "This is what I (or we) have found." From this it follows, of course, that the common form of this conversation should be narrative. Stories should be a constant presence in the classroom of the religious educator. Stories from the teacher's life, stories of other important people, biblical stories, stories of the saints: all these should give vitality to the process of education. Indeed, to put this another way, the first audience to which the teacher speaks should be the imagination of the students, not the intellect. When intellect is addressed (as it eventually should be), this should serve to explain what has already been experienced in the outer world or in imagination, not to substitute for that experience.

Third, this focus on imagination reminds us that the media of communication should be both diverse and creative. In recent years religious educators have become much more adept at using visual media. There are many wonderful videos prepared for the use of catechists, and to the teacher with imagination, endless possibilities reside in commercial movies and television shows. What we have learned about the centrality of imagination simply explains why these approaches are so well suited to the project of inviting discipleship. In the religious education of the future they should be emphasized even more.

Fourth, since the power of the values resides in the group, communication should be lateral as well as centrifugal. That is, the communication should pass among the participants, and not just from the central teacher to the peripheral audience. To the teacher who understands the process of value formation, group discussion is not a tactic employed to fill a class period with insufficient content. Rather, it is a pivotal component of a process intended to build on experience, to touch imagination, to cultivate relationship, and thus to transform identity.

Rote

These reflections prompt me to add another comment, one which may seem surprising. I want to highlight the "role of rote." There was a time when much of religious education involved memorization. In any Catholic parish one can still find a significant number of people whose education was shaped by the *Baltimore Catechism,* with its series of brief questions and answers memorized by the students and presented to the teacher on command. More recently, a reaction to this excessive reliance on rote has led to an educational approach in which it has almost no place. Our research suggests a middle road.

Albert Bandura's analysis of modeling emphasized the need to get the attention of the one to be influenced. That might seem obvious, but Bandura reminded us that focused attention is not always easy to achieve. Memorization can serve the modest but important role of encouraging attention. Being able to recite the Lord's Prayer does not guarantee that it is meant. But being able to recite it at least means that the speaker is in a position to *consider* meaning it. And to the extent that the words are icons for a way of life and a vision of reality, to that extent the speaker is in a position to observe and maybe even to imitate.

Similarly, Samuel Oliner reported that people behave in ways that express the norms of their group. But how is an individual to know the norms of the group? Memorization provides the student with a clear summary of those norms. At the same time, the group's call for the memorization, if it is authentic, symbolizes its real commitment to those norms. An example will highlight this value of memorization—and its limits.

I believe it makes good sense to ask young people to memorize the Ten Commandments. I do not presume that the commandments adequately summarize all that is involved in discipleship, but it is a concise summary of the outer limits of appropriate behavior in this community. I also do not presume that the commandments involve the technical language needed to resolve honest ethical dilemmas. (Does "Thou shalt not kill" reject all killing or just that unjust killing known as murder?) Indeed, biblical scholars tell us that the text of the Ten Commandments is a poem, composed for recitation in liturgical settings, much like the *Gloria* or the *Credo* of the Mass. Still a concise summary, perhaps especially a poetic summary, can serve to focus attention on the challenges of faithful living in a community of faith. Indeed, inasmuch as poetry is a thing of beauty and not just of conceptual truth, to that extent poetic summaries can speak to the imagination and not just to the intellect.

But the whole process is for naught if these standards do not actually guide the behavior of the group. If the commandment charges truth telling while it is obvious that the community indulges in falsehood, then the memorized text will fall on deaf ears. For as we have already seen, whenever there is contradiction between the languages of word and of body, the listener will believe the body language.

So the religious educator seeking to invite discipleship need not apologize for a judicious use of memorization. In fact, if we understand religious education as also a process of inculturation into a group, the learning of treasured texts can establish another identity-shaping bond. But none of this will work if it is not fundamentally true. The words must speak the community's truth, and the community must confirm in the language of its corporate body the claims it makes in its corporate texts.

Practice

In fact, so important is this body language, that we can envision a sort of "embodied rote" activity. It goes by the name of "practice." In his analysis of the process of modeling, Albert Bandura also showed that success in this process requires that its recipient actually try the proposed behavior. This enactment of behavioral alternatives, even when it is done with less than total personal commitment, can have the effect of liberating the person from past limitations into a realm of new possibilities.

No doubt this is one of the reasons that concrete activities have taken an increasingly prominent role in religious education. Another reason, of course, is that all learning must in some way be experience-based, since only experience can transform the moral sensibilities out of which our concrete choices are made. In any case, there is hardly a confirmation program to be found that does not include a service project as an important component.

Similarly, at my university, and surely at many others, an important part of the program of campus ministry is played by a selection of "immersion opportunities." Students travel to other situations, often other countries, and experience first hand the struggles in which people of good will are engaged, the sufferings they are forced to endure, and the beauty with which they persevere. There is no illusion that the students will change anything in the setting to which they travel. No, the change envisioned is a change in the students. And if this happens, then maybe also there will someday be a change in the students' local situation, resisting those almost-unnoticed local injustices that make the far-off suffering of others inevitable.

Even in the classroom, religious educators who understand deeply the process of value formation, work to provide experiential opportunities. Role-playing games, laboratory work, deeply felt interactions with one another: all these provide an opportunity for the participants to practice the disciple's way of life. Through that practice, opportunities for personal growth are multiplied and reinforced.

Virtue

These many reflections can be summarized and concluded by returning to a theme that has achieved increasing prominence in recent moral theology. We have seen that "virtue" involves both the inclination and the ability to behave in a certain way. So the project of inviting discipleship can equally be understood as a project of cultivating virtue, for it is a project in which we try to stimulate a sincere inclination to live in the way of Jesus. At the same time it is a project in which we try to provide opportunities for encounter and exploration, imitation and practice which will nurture the ability to do precisely that.

In focusing on virtue, moreover, we are focusing more on person than on particular acts. And rightly so, since we realize that people live out of their identities. But for that very reason, we can also summarize our task as the development of Christian character, following the lead of Stanley Hauerwas and other theologians.

I am intrigued by the increasing attention that these perspectives have been receiving recently. A wide range of secular writing, not particularly interested in cultivating Christian discipleship but deeply committed to improving the moral climate of our culture, is turning from norms to character, from behavior to personal identity. The Josephson Institute, for example, has attempted to influence society by identifying several key "virtues" on which widespread consensus is possible. Work with focus groups led to the naming of six qualities or, as they call them, "pillars of character": trustworthiness, respect, responsibility, fairness, caring, and citizenship. They have gone on to develop programming designed to inculcate these virtues in young people, gathering this programming under the notable title *Character Counts.* They have even mobilized the power of imagination by developing an animated video and composing a series of children's songs entitled "Kids for Character."[3] Other organizations are pursuing similar avenues. So should all of us interested in religious education.

But if the notions of character and virtue provide a focus for the efforts of religious education, they also prompt a call for humility. For in watching the motion picture of an individual life, the character of the central character (as it is curiously called) is not fully revealed in a single scene nor, even less, in a snapshot caught at a random moment. Only at the end of the movie will the truth of the person be revealed, for that truth is both composed of and influenced by all the episodes that comprise the story. So it will be with us.

Over the last couple of years I have joined with several relatives in seeking to help a particular young man. He had done poorly in high school, neither achieving academic success nor participating in the many activities that help the maturation process. But he claimed to have learned from the experience and sought a new opportunity. So we worked to arrange a way for him to attend a junior college, providing a living situation, making available a financial subsidy, offering counsel, and the like.

For a while things went well. But in the end he did not succeed. Indeed, he did not even persevere in the effort to succeed, choosing instead to quit school, give up a well-paying job, and move in with a young woman of recent acquaintance. In his own words, he was tired of the waiting and the work. He was ready for life to start now.

You will not be surprised to know that all of us who contributed to this young man's opportunity are left with feelings of disappointment, sadness, even anger. But we also know that we cannot allow these feelings to fill the picture. Good things happened over the course of this year. This young man was exposed to a series of excellent models; he shared deepening experiences; he encountered alternative visions of life; he heard words of loving challenge and of genuine care. And those things do not disappear. If we were not able to overcome some quite unhelpful models from his past, nor his lack of practice in the art of discipline, nor those peculiar physical drives that are adolescence, it does not follow that we did nothing. And the movie is not over.

Conclusion

So we must cast our contribution like bread upon the water and hope that it will nourish the spirit at an unknown time and in an unknown way. Yes, we must hope—and we must pray. I began this chapter by defining religious education as that set of activities that systematically exposes people to the convictions of the Christian community in such a manner that they are invited to—even encouraged to—embrace the life of discipleship. But inviting and encouraging are not the same as creating. And when it comes to the reality of discipleship, the act of creation resides in the hands of God.

As St. Paul reminded the Corinthians, "I planted, Apollos watered, but God gave the growth" (1 Cor. 3:6). Indeed, this personal experience of mine teaches that the success of our efforts to impact positively the lives of our human fellows is always in God's hands. But most certainly and most especially is this true in the case of religious education, where the envisioned positive contribution is nothing less than a disciple's relationship with the Lord of Life, the Savior of us all, and the Spirit who sets all free.

And that is why the title of this chapter is "Inviting Discipleship." If in faith we dare do no less, it is equally true that in love we can do no more.[4]

Notes

1. A splendid example of the use of quality theology in the development of pastoral practice is William Bausch, *A Total Parish Manual* (Mystic, Conn.:

Twenty Third Publications, 1994). I have not directly used Bausch's work in developing these chapters, but my many positive memories of his book have made it something of a model for what follows.

2. The central role played in religious education by the relationship of student and teacher is explored by Andrew M. Greeley, *The Religious Imagination* (New York: Sadlier, 1981), especially pp. 63–72. As in much of his work, Greeley here grounds his reflections on careful sociological research.

3. Further information on all these materials may be received from the Josephson Institute of Ethics, 4640 Admiralty Way, Suite 1001, Marina del Rey, CA 90292.

4. This approach to religious education is hardly unique with me. Among the many scholars who have encouraged perspectives like this, special mention should be made of Thomas H. Groome, *Sharing Faith* (San Francisco: Harper-SanFrancisco, 1991).

13

Celebrating Discipleship

THE CONSTITUTION ON THE SACRED LITURGY OF VATICAN II
asserted that "the liturgy is the summit toward which the activity of the
Church is directed; at the same time it is the fountain from which her
power flows,"[1] or, as it is often put, the "source and summit of the
Church's life." Yet for many Catholics it is no such thing. Travel
around the United States, slip into parish churches from Charleston to
Seattle, and the experience will be distressingly similar: boredom, distraction, routine. Even those who believe in the liturgical reforms
often despair at the half-hearted implementation of the council's proposals. And those who never did believe in the reforms find in current
liturgical practice ample proof that the sense of mystery and awe, the
soul-touching power that is the center of true worship, has been generally lost.

I have no interest in joining the debate about whether the proposals
of the council were wrongheaded. On the one hand, every grousing
tale of today's liturgical miseries can be matched by a horror story of
times gone by. And on the other hand, if the "old liturgy" had true
power, the sources of that power can be set into today's formularies just
as well. The character of good liturgy—and of bad liturgy—transcends
the details of the particular ceremonies.

So my interest is drawn toward enlivening liturgy for our time.
Everything that we have learned in these pages about the making of
disciples can be applied to our lives of worship, with the result that the
liturgical rituals in which we engage will indeed be both the source and
summit of that Christian life of discipleship to which all are called.

Liturgical Triangle

Good liturgy, it seems to me, involves three components, word, music, and gesture. Each is important, and none may be neglected. Moreover, all three components interconnect and mutually reinforce one another, such that they must all be considered in concert. The image, I would contend, is of a triangle, each of these components at a point, all contributing strength. When the components are in balance and when all are providing their contribution, the result is that dynamic trinitarian phenomenon that is genuine, authentic, transformative, and inspiring liturgy. When they are not, the result is the mess we so often endure.

My experience is that liturgical planning, at least in the United States, has made its best effort in the area of music. Careful attention to the proclamation of words, and even more to the body language of the rituals, has been almost universally lacking. But none of these aspects has been engaged as deeply as necessary. And since successful liturgy (which, to my mind, is synonymous with "genuine liturgy") occurs only when all three get the attention they deserve, it will be worthwhile to give each its consideration in this chapter.[2]

Words of Life

If all liturgical participants were to be polled on their reasons for attendance, I suspect that the most common response would be to "receive communion." Perhaps even "because we're supposed to!" But when people are invited to talk in some detail about their experience of the liturgy, it is not long before they offer comments on the words of the ceremony. They critique the homily. They complain that they could not understand the readers. They note the rushed pace that manifests clearly the absence of meaning for the speaker, as surely as for the listener.

I confess to being dumbfounded by many of the liturgical sins against the word. It seems to me self-evident that words are meant to communicate, and yet communication is often woefully absent. For those of us who are willing to repent, I offer the following suggestions.

First, let us make sure we always mean what we say. Perhaps you have traveled by air recently. Do you remember the flight attendant's tone of voice during the required announcements? "Touching, tampering, or disabling a smoke detector is prohibited by law and violators will be prosecuted. . . ." (You must try to hear those words in the way they were spoken.) Have you ever wondered if the attendant was speaking some language other than English? The pace, the inflection, the sing-song tone: all these reveal clearly that not a word is actually meant!

The same thing is sadly true of many liturgical speeches. The presider announces: "Let us pray," and evidently wants no such thing. The reader asks us to pray to the Lord for the sick and suffering, and apparently knows only of the hale and hardy. And we righteous ones, occupying our pews, we give every indication that the words "hallowed be thy name" come from some long dead and utterly alien language. There is no subtle technique involved here, no trick known only to Shakespearean actors. The challenge is simple: mean what you say and say what you mean!

But this challenge cannot be enacted instantaneously. I need time to compose myself for honest speech. So the second point, a complement to the first, is this: till the soil of speech with spades of silence. I am amazed at the sanctity of my fellow worshipers in many congregations; apparently they are ready to respond from the heart the very second that a scriptural reading ends! At least that is what is suggested by the immediate beginning of the responsorial psalm or song. For my part, I need a minute to think about what I've heard. Is it completely grumpy of me to conclude from the pace of all this that I am not *really* expected to think about the reading nor, for that matter, to *really* respond from my heart? And in the case where the response is musical (as it should be), is it horribly judgmental of me to suspect that the musician wasn't even listening to the reading?

The story is told of a Native American engaging in dialogue with a European American. Their communication was not short on misunderstandings; indeed offense was taken more than once. As they eventually became friends and were able to name the problems, one stood out. "Many times," said the Native American, "you would begin to speak the minute I concluded. You even interrupted. If you were really listening to me, how could your response be so quickly prepared? It was obvious to me that you were not listening. No, a posture of attention disguised an act of composition." Listening, thinking, responding: these are three different activities. True respect for our words requires that we leave time in our liturgy for each of them.

Yet one more thing is required, so obvious that mere mention of it embarrasses. We need to speak in such a way that we can be heard! In today's church there is much talk of "ministries." Exactly what activities fall under this title is a subject of debate. But no one disagrees that the various services provided by particular members of the liturgical assembly are ministries. This is an important point, for it is often noted that no one has a *right* to exercise ministry. Rather, individuals need to be *called* to the ministry by the community, and this call should, in turn, be grounded in the individual's possession of a *charism*, or skill, for the ministry being considered. Why is that? Because ministries are services to the community, and the community should assure itself that service will truly be provided in each individual case.

Thus, to state what should be obvious, the only persons who should be proclaiming the readings are those with the ability to proclaim them, and communicate them, effectively. Do they have the physical ability to project the sounds? Are they able to articulate the words with clarity and precision? Is there sufficient understanding so that the text can come alive with meaning? To put this simply: Will a congregation open to sincere listening be allowed to truly hear "the Word of the Lord"?

Homilies

If all this is true of each of the words of liturgy, it is especially true of the high profile words that comprise the homily. It is not uncommon to take easy pot-shots at homilists, decrying the level of preaching in our time. I confess that I have participated in this talk. But then, one beautiful spring day, I attended the high school graduation of my nephew. The featured speaker was a local banker, a prominent figure in the town, evidently a bright and personable man. And his speech? One of the most dismal examples of public discourse I have ever heard! And as I endured this seemingly endless disquisition, the thought struck me: it isn't easy, speaking in public. Religious preachers, individuals who in many ways are quite ordinary people, are daring to engage in a singularly daunting activity. To have something worthwhile to say, to say it clearly, and to be effective in communication: this is a most challenging assignment. So perhaps the amazing thing is not that the preaching is not better than it is, but rather that it is not worse than it is. That graduation day, I resolved to reserve a corner of my heart for respect and appreciation for all who endeavor to preach.

But in saying all this, I don't mean to settle for the level of preaching often experienced. The project of presenting effectively and endearingly the gospel of the Lord is too important for that. Rather, I want to serve the good-hearted preachers among us by naming some of the lessons suggested by the research in these pages, suggestions that can make preaching significantly better.

A public-speaking teacher with whom I once studied put it this way: every good sermon should have one good point and two good stories. Let us consider each item in turn.

Every homily should have a point. Not a collection of points, not a vague universe of insight; rather a single, focused point. After all, a homily is by definition a relatively brief speech, and in five to ten minutes, only one point can be effectively communicated. This teacher required us to state our point; he insisted it be formulated in a single sentence, with no subordinate clauses. This is not easy. Not only is the precision of mind a challenge, the process of selection is equally daunting. For the simple fact is that any of the Gospel selections assigned for Sunday Eucharists invites the addressing of a wide range of points. So perhaps the homilist's greatest challenge, the asceticism of the role, is to acknowledge a plate full of ideas, all worthy of exploration, but all save one postponed to another day.

Next, said this teacher, clothe that one point in two stories. What an important insight this is! A homily is a particular art form. It is not an intellectual exercise addressed to the minds of the listeners. Rather, it is an inspirational exercise, addressed to their hearts. The goal of the homily is not clarity; the goal of the homily is conversion. Ideas that are intellectually stimulating are not necessarily out of order, of course; but they must justify themselves by their service to the listeners' change of heart. And for this project it is the stories that hold center stage, not the point.

I have heard many presentations from a pulpit that were not homilies. Rather they were cogent articulations of themes that would have well suited a homily, had one ever been written. In other words, many preachers stop at the first step, identifying their point. They do not realize that, with that point, they have traveled only half-way home. They have not moved on to the project of crafting this thing of beauty, this message to the heart, that a true homily always is.

It is at this point, and here alone, that I part company with my teacher of long ago. He made us declare our single point and then tell our two appropriate stories. Today I would advise the preacher: skip the point, just tell the stories! This advice may be a bit extreme, but it clarifies the essential point. Homilies speak to the heart; and the heart's language is poetry, image, and metaphor, story, rhythm, and flow.

Music

No doubt further comments could be made on the project of presenting living words within the liturgy. But let's move on to the second leg of good liturgy: music. It is here that I find it most difficult to form suggestions that will be helpful to all. For as I travel around the United States, I am astonished at the huge range of musical expressions, different not only in their aesthetic styles but also in their liturgical pertinence.

At one parish I will encounter simple settings of the Holy and the Great Amen, chant-like refrains to the Responsorial Psalm. But I can feel the way these tunes carry the prayer of this congregation, how they are sung with pride and comfort and sincerity. At another parish I will experience recited Psalms and Acclamations standing next to an "Offertory Song" (despite the fact that there is no such part of the Mass and that the Preparation of the Gifts is among the least important aspects of the liturgy) whose text has absolutely no connection to the feast being celebrated. The difference between the parishes does not seem to be financial resources or physical equipment. As best I can tell, there is no difference except thoughtfulness.

So I will not pad these reflections with comments that can be found by anyone willing to read the official books or to encounter good musical liturgy in the many places it exists. I will simply make a few comments that arise from the research of this book.

First, we know that values reside in the feelings of the person. It follows that the pathway to value is the pathway of the affect. Music, they say, can tame the savage beast. It can also raise the mind and heart to God like little else. That is why it is thrilling to note the growing library of beautiful and tasteful music being composed for the liturgy. It has taken us thirty years to begin to *feel* how music connects to the liturgy of Vatican II, but from the viewpoint of history thirty years is not a long time.

Second, we know that values reside as much in communities as in individuals, such that people live out of the values of the communities in which they are invested. It follows that if liturgy is to touch and transform the values of the individual, it must express and envision the values of the community. That is why it is encouraging to note the multiplication of beautiful pieces of music that combine the singing of the whole community with contributions from those of particular talent. The increased use of refrains, the more complex interweavings of congregation, choir, and instruments of various kinds: all these are evident. Now, for example, we have perhaps eight to ten beautiful settings of the Eucharistic Prayer, all designed to incorporate the active participation of the praying community with the leading prayer of the priest. Often the talented singing of a choir adds richness, as different instruments help build to what truly can be called a "Great Amen." The result is shared prayer that thrills the heart and stirs it to adoration.

Finally, our appreciation of the ways in which spirit and body interact has led to a renaissance of music for meditation. In many places we are past the point where choir and congregation are viewed adversarially. We realize that we are all congregation, and we serve one another by the offer of our particular gifts. Allowing oneself to be carried on music as we listen—this is also a gift. For this stirring of the sensibilities connects intimately to the prayerful acts of the disciple's spirit.

Gesture

We come now to the third point on the liturgical triangle, and I must say at the outset that in my experience it is the most neglected and abused dimension of the liturgy. If the amount of time and energy devoted within liturgical planning is any indication, most planners see human beings as speaking, singing angels. The language of the body, they seem to believe, is unimportant if not actually unreal.

Yet we know this is not true. If anything, body language is primary, so that if there is discrepancy between that language and our words, the listener will decide it is the words that are false. Hence, in order that liturgy may actually celebrate and nurture the life of discipleship, nothing is more important than increased intention to the declarations that we embody in its celebrations.

I will offer a simple example. During the eucharistic song known as the Lamb of God, the presider breaks the consecrated host. Later, as the communion service is being introduced, some presiders actually attempt to rejoin the pieces, holding up for view an unbroken large round host. Many presiders then proceed to consume that host, a piece of consecrated bread that is perhaps five times as large as that offered to each of the other communicants. What does this say? Surely it says that the presider is more important than the other members of the congregation. It also says, or at least suggests, that his sharing is some-how more central to the reality of the Eucharist and that their sharing is somehow peripheral.

Most presiders do not intentionally wish to say this, of course. But they do. And this is all the more curious since the rubrics, those regu-lations that are often viewed as "conservative," call for quite a different message. "The eucharistic bread . . . should therefore be made in such a way that the priest can break it and distribute the parts to at least some of the faithful. When the number of communicants is large . . . small hosts may be used."[3] These words suggest a more egalitarian vision of this ritual. On the one hand, small hosts are really nothing other than large hosts that have been broken in advance with the assis-tance of technology. On the other hand, the breaking of the large host occurring during the Lamb of God should result in even more pieces of similar size. Once that breaking is completed, there is no suggestion that any particular particle belongs to the priest nor that the portion consumed by the priest should be in any way distinguishable from those offered to the members of the congregation. So in this case the body language commonly communicated in parochial practice is not only unfortunate, it is also officially unsupported.

On numerous occasions I have used this example, and the response has been interesting. When I have spoken to priests, I have often been accused (in a friendly fashion, of course) of "making a mountain out of a mole hill." "No one even notices that sort of thing," said one priest. But when I have shared this example with lay people, they have reported a high degree of awareness. "Thank God you're saying this," said one listener. "That's been bugging me for years!"

As I mentioned above, very few priests, if any, actually intend to pro-ject an insulting and alienating message. So my point is not that some presiders lack love for their people. Rather, the point is simply that body language is powerful, that it is rarely unnoticed, and that as a con-sequence those who wish to celebrate discipleship must consider it carefully.

Think of the message of the space itself. In the renovation of one church the moment came for selecting carpeting for the "sanctuary." The rest of the church was floored in an elegant grey tile. Should the carpeting have a contrasting color? After much conversation the answer was negative. "We want the eye to be able to focus on the action," they said. "But we do not want to telegraph the assertion that this is a 'separate space.' In fact, the entire church is the sanctuary." So they chose a tasteful grey carpet that blended gently with the rest of the flooring. In another church the persons responsible for decorations take care that banners, flowers, and the like are located throughout the worship space and not just by the altar. For this arrangement, they believe, more accurately incarnates the church's teaching that the Eucharist is a common celebration of the whole people of God.

Think of the language of specific gestures. It is not easy to find gestures that are reasonably comfortable for a particular group while still sufficiently "uncomfortable" that they speak with power, but it can be done. The rubrics call for all to bow during the central words of the Nicene Creed. For some reason this gesture has not been adopted by many people. At the same time, I find it more and more common that congregations raise their hand in shared blessing over the newly baptized, those being confirmed, newlyweds, and the like. It is a gesture that "grabs" one; one simply cannot remain unengaged while doing something like this. And yet people seem willing to do it.

Would that liturgical planners would give equivalent attention to all the other dimensions of gesture. What posture do the people take for particular moments in the Mass? Where do the various ministers sit? Do readers come from the congregation or do they remain near the side of the presider? Do we assure that the ranks of the ministers for each ceremony accurately reflect the diversity of the entire congregation, visually presenting *this* congregation in miniature?

Other Examples

Think of other moments when deeply important statements could better be made nonverbally. A cloistered community of sisters once elected to celebrate an entire Eucharist in which they would say nothing. They did not stop responding, they simply replaced words with gestures. Thus, when the priest extended his hands while saying, "The Lord be with you," they simply extended their hands in response. The event was a bit extreme, even eccentric. The sisters did not express a desire to celebrate in this way often. But they were moved by the experience, led to embrace more deeply those words that can too easily become rote.

In one parish, the gathering of the collection has been formalized. (I can't help being amused at the surreptitious, almost apologetic way in which it is taken in most places.) The gifts of bread and wine are brought forward. As they are held high, the congregation stands and likewise holds in their hands the gifts they are offering. A brief refrain is sung. Then, as the priest prepares the altar, the people's gifts are gathered. In another parish, the communal celebration of the Sacrament of Reconciliation on occasion involves a procession in which the penitents come forward and by a solemn wordless gesture of genuflection confess their sinfulness. The priest then proclaims over each one the traditional words of absolution.[4] In many parishes baptisms are enriched by a procession in which all those present impose the sign of the cross upon the one being baptized.

Finally, the community with which I regularly celebrate has developed a moving custom for the Good Friday liturgy. The rubrically mandated veneration of the cross occurs at the usual place in the ceremony, but according to the brief communal version, which the rubrics permit. Then after communion the priest prays that final prayer which provides this liturgy its odd "conclusion without ending." But the congregation is urged to remain for a few moments of private prayer and then, when they are ready to depart, to come forward to the cross to offer a personal gesture of veneration. Any gesture is acceptable, so long as it comes from the heart of the individual.

What follows is a powerful experience, for observers as well as actors. Some simply bow. Many kiss the cross. Some genuflect. One young man with dark skin that suggested Arabic background went to his knees and slowly bowed his head, touching his forehead to the ground. Many reach out with a gentle, intimate touch that obviously carries a message of the heart. Tears are not at all uncommon. For in this wordless moment, that deeper human language is allowed a wondrous range of speech.

Conclusion

Liturgy is the celebration of discipleship, expressing the way to which believers have committed themselves. It is also, and concomitantly, an enactment of that discipleship which also deepens the commitment of all involved. But to be what it is, liturgy must be authentic. That is, it must be true and honest, and it must belong to those who participate, speaking their language and expressing their faith. And that authenticity must apply to all three of liturgy's dimensions, to its words, to its music, and to its gestures. When authenticity is lacking in any of the dimensions, liturgy limps and people are impoverished. When it is present, the power of religious ritual is wondrously manifest.

Because of this, I have highlighted with details the challenge of authentic words, music, and gesture. But as these reflections are concluded one final point should be made. And it is this: the foundation for the power of liturgy is its very existence.

I was once asked to present a talk on the topic "The Liturgy and Morality." When I accepted the invitation, I fully intended to share ideas about how liturgy could support specific moral convictions and commitments without degenerating into empty moralism or judgmental abuse. But as I reflected in the process of preparing my remarks, I came to realize that it was the very coming together for worship, the very existence of the liturgical community, that was its most powerful moral statement.

We claim to be disciples of the Lord, and in one sense we truly are. But surely all of us would admit the partiality of our discipleship, the ways in which it is contradicted by selfishness or weakness or confusion. So while discipleship is our possession, it is also always our destination. And what helps us arrive at that destination? It is the existence of the liturgical community.

I come to Mass some Sundays like a thirsty man crawling from the desert into an oasis. What if there is no water? Then I am a dead man. What if, on this Sunday, there is no community of discipleship to which I can attach myself? I am just as surely dead. But for many of us, that is happily not the case. We enter a liturgical assembly that nourishes us. Our commitment to discipleship and our understanding of its demands are renewed. How is that done? Through words, and music, and gesture, to be sure. But most profoundly, through the community itself.

In our weakness we come into a community of faith. Not an angelic community, to be sure, nor a community of saints, but a community of those who, like me, were at least willing to take the step of being present. It is a community that cares enough about their faith to bring their children, who may run and play, being distracted and distracting others as children always do, but who are present nonetheless. It is a community that may recite prayers too automatically and hesitate to sing and feel awkward at some gestures, but which does participate nonetheless. It is a community that greets me with peace and seems to mean it, that consumes the food that brings communion with the Lord and one another and seems to treasure it, that chooses to spend part of Sunday in an activity that is as optional as anything in our society and seems not to regret it.

So by this community I too am nourished. In the Lord the community and I become one. The community's values become, at least a little more, my values. The community's way of life reveals itself, at least a little more, in my way of life. And as I share the community's prayers and absorb the community's dreams, we together do again what followers of Jesus have done since the very beginning.

We become one in celebrating discipleship.

Notes

1. "Constitution on the Sacred Liturgy," §10, in *The Documents of Vatican II*, ed. Walter Abbott (New York: Herder & Herder, 1966), 142.

2. My focus will be the eucharistic liturgy, and indeed, the Sunday Eucharist, since that is the event at which the greatest numbers are present. But all of these comments would pertain as well to the other liturgies, both sacramental celebrations and prayer services of various kinds. Indeed, I believe the worship forms of other Christian traditions can equally benefit from these considerations. For they serve not Roman Catholic liturgy as such, but the act of genuine worship which discipleship demands of all.

3. General Instruction of the Roman Missal, §283.

4. This arrangement may seem at first glance to be unorthodox. But church teaching is clear that only those in mortal sin are obliged to confess by species and number. All others are obliged only to confess their sinfulness, and there is no regulation requiring that this be done verbally. Also, as long as the ceremonial includes both individual confession of sinfulness and individual absolution, the celebration constitutes a legitimate variation and not the much-ballyhooed "general absolution." For a full discussion of the theological and legal issues surrounding ceremonies of Reconciliation, see Timothy O'Connell, "Reconciliation Renewal: Healing For Today's Church," *Chicago Studies* 32 (1993): 114–26.

14

Living Discipleship

SINCE THE BEGINNING, FOLLOWERS OF JESUS HAVE FORMED among themselves a community of disciples. Given everything we now know about the social nature of the human person, this is not surprising, for affiliation is a universal human tendency. But the community formed by disciples is a very particular sort of community, and the name for this community is "church."

An interesting item from Catholic theology is the conviction that "church" exists fully in each of the local churches, or dioceses, as they are called. Thus, individual dioceses are not "branch offices" of a church centrally existing in Rome. Rather, they are each "church," a community of disciples; and in their unity of faith, they are all also "church" together.

In today's world, however, even a diocese is generally too large to locate the experience of shared discipleship. So I want to turn our attention instead to "parish" as the place where people must encounter and live their identity as a community of disciples. And in this last chapter of reflections on the research that we have explored, I want to ask the question, What can we learn from this research about living discipleship in the local parish?

I believe that this research provides four suggestions for parish life in the church today. It says that parish should be a place of gifts and a place of groups, a place of stories and a place of standards. Let's consider each of these in turn.

Place of Gifts

As I write this chapter, a new bishop has just begun his service to the Catholic diocese of Chicago. In various opening statements, he has proposed as a priority efforts to bring back to church those who have "fallen away." I suppose that this is a worthy objective, but it raises an important question: Why would I return to active participation in church? The answer strikes me as obvious: I would return because church participation somehow enriches me, because I find my needs met there, because, in a word, I experience church as a place of gifts. So it is important for us to ask: In what way is church a place of gifts? What needs does it meet?

Sadly, this question will strike some people as inappropriate. I have rarely heard pastors focus on the needs that are met in their parishes. Conversely, I have often heard them focus on people's *obligation* to participate. But whether or not people actually have that obligation, the fact is that people join and remain in communities that meet their needs. As the sociologists have taught us, people become committed to groups that are genuinely salient to them. That is, when people experience a group as truly important, such that desirable things would be lost if one disaffiliated, such that elements of one's identity would be threatened by departure, then and only then do they embrace the group and set down roots.

So pastoral ministers need to look at their people and ask the question, What needs of these people do we meet? If the parish is successful, they should be able to identify several.

First, there are the simplest of human needs: affectivity and affiliation. We have seen that the world of values is an affective world, more a matter of the heart than of the head. Hence any community committed to the mediation of values must be a place of affectivity. Look at the parish and ask: Is this a place of warmth? It saddens me how outrageous this question must seem when asked in certain settings. In my own travels I have often slipped into a church to attend Mass. Sometimes I am struck by the coldness of the setting, a chill of emotional temperature if not physical. I see no smiles, I hear no laughter. The people do not look at one another. No one conveys the sense that they are glad to be there. I cannot help wondering why, in the end, they remain.

In contrast to this, I have often noticed a quite delightful tone. I observe people waving to one another. I see the pastoral ministers standing at the door, greeting people with interest and enthusiasm. The homily invites a chuckle, perhaps even a tear. There is a comfortable warmth that makes one glad to be involved.

Immediately connected to this affectivity is affiliation. I do not mean that the members of a parish are all best friends. They clearly are not. But the thousands of persons who attend sporting events are not best friends either, yet they are most certainly affiliated.[1] The same thing is true of parish. When I observe the parishioners in these warm and affectionate parishes, I can almost sense the dotted lines that connect them. Between them are bonds, not walls.

I refer here to "temperature," the warmth of the emotional experience, not of the building itself. But we have learned to take seriously the embodiedness of the human person. So I am not surprised at the connections between these two sorts of temperature. Many years ago I noticed one of the most common differences between Catholic churches and those of some other denominations: the non-Catholic churches had coat rooms! A small thing, it seems. But upon reflection this difference struck me as highly significant. It is amazing how often the participants at Mass not only do not hang up their coats, they do not even take them off. Imagine what it would do to the tone of a family dinner if the participants left on their coats. The body language would certainly be negative. "I'm not staying," it would say. "I'm just passing through." What a difference it would make if parishioners could be convinced to "take off their coats and stay awhile"!

So the parish should be a place where one finds the gifts of affectivity and affiliation. Second, it should be a place that offers the gift of support. That is, it should be a place where one receives help with the many struggles of human life. Struggles like raising one's children. In one parish of my acquaintance the staff sponsored a group called PITS, Parents of Infants and Toddlers! In this group the parents received wonderful support dealing with the demands of little children. I have seen the same thing when the parents of teenagers are brought together. For many people the greatest challenge, and most important project, of their lives is the raising of their children. Surely the parish should be a place where one is helped in that project.

Support can also be offered at times of special trouble. Certainly ministry to the bereaved is an important service of parish. But also ministry to those who have lost their job, endured financial setbacks, experienced the pain of divorce, suffered the abandonment that is so often the fate of the elderly. And support can be offered to those whose circumstances pose abiding challenges. I think of members of racial, social, or sexual minorities, people with chronic illness and their caregivers, the physically, mentally, or emotionally handicapped, and those struggling to achieve sobriety or to live lives of recovery. In a parish that is a place of gifts, the need for personal support in life's projects will regularly be met.

Third, the parish should meet the need for meaning. Human life is filled with engaging experiences that distract us from ultimate questions of meaning. When I am surrounded by those I love, when my projects meet with success, when my health is strong and my mind is quick: when all this is true, I suffer no crisis of meaning. These experiences are gifts of God too, of course, and in the end they also nourish the search for meaning. But they do not make the demand for meaning inescapable; quite the contrary, they allow it to be avoided.

It has been said that any theology worthy of the name is a theology of catastrophe. That is, it is only when it becomes clear that I am not God that my need for God asserts itself. It is only when the experience of failure reveals itself as the central part of life which death confirms it is, that we must confront the question of what comes after. At those moments, then, the moments of death and of those lesser catastrophes that foreshadow death, the search for meaning begins. And any parish worthy of the name must minister to that search. Through aptly chosen words, through tender rituals, through the grace of quiet presence, the gift of meaning must be offered.

In all these circumstances the parish should be a place of gifts, a place where important human needs are met. For only in this way will the parish become a place that is truly important to the participants who comprise it.

Place of Groups

The story is told of a certain pastor, famous for his success in leading a parish. The presumption was that he had all sorts of skills. But when a curious fellow priest began to investigate, he discovered a most amazing thing.

There was the time when a parishioner approached this pastor.

"Father," he said, "you have got to do something for the teens. They are terribly neglected in this parish, and it's just not right."

"You're absolutely right," responded the pastor, "and I would gladly work with the teens, if I could. Unfortunately, I'm just no good at working with young people. But if you would be willing to take charge, I will happily help and support you."

Some time later, the Director of Religious Education spoke to the pastor. "Father, we have a problem. The catechists feel unequipped for their work because they're not very clear on Catholic doctrine. Would you teach a course to them?"

"Oh, I'd love to do that for you," said the pastor, "but you can't believe what a terrible teacher I am. Why don't we bring in someone really good at that? I'll write the letter inviting the catechists, and I'll certainly attend all the sessions. But could you put it together?"

Slowly the pattern became clear. This pastor didn't do *anything*. Rather he supported and encouraged the initiatives of other people. He allowed them to take center stage while he remained quietly and caringly in the background. It was the parish that was the true success: that's what the priest investigator learned. But for that very reason, the pastor was a success as well.

This story embodies an important lesson. Everything that we have learned in these pages confirms that values are transmitted through groups. Consequently, the creation and fostering of groups are central to the mission of parish. Not only the overall group that is the parish itself, but also myriad smaller groups convened out of need and maintained out of conviction.

Recently I shared dinner with a long-time friend. We talked of many things, catching up on our "doings," for it had been a long time since we were last together. In due course, the conversation turned to the death of his father some months before. I commented on the wonderful outpouring of support at the funeral. He agreed, describing how touched he had been by the many personal and professional acquaintances who had been present. He talked of the strength this group had offered to his family and himself.

These thoughts led him to talk about his family, and that, in turn, led gently to his describing for me the final days of his father's life. I sat silent but profoundly attentive as he offered to my mind's eye their experience of sharing. I saw how close they were, and how much closer they became. I marveled at how his father's courage stimulated greatness in everyone. Important words of love and release were spoken. Gentle, unselfconscious gestures were shared. Presence was offered and received. Most importantly, the gift of faith was received from one another as, paradoxically, it was offered to one another. It was, in this mutual sharing, professed together and so became a rock of strength. My sense of the beauty of these moments was confirmed when my friend described how nurses and staff joined them around their father's deathbed, so inspired were they by what was happening, so touched were they by the sight of what faith made possible.

As my friend shared these intimate, inspiring recollections, tears came to his eyes, and they came to my eyes as well. There, in the midst of that restaurant, with a strange sort of safety, a sort of gentle anonymity, we wept at the sadness and the beauty of it all.

And now, as I think back to that dinner, I am struck by the lesson of our sharing: the fact that we humans only truly live in the groups with which we share identity and experience. My friend and I were a group that evening. The family that he described in his recollections was a group of the most wondrously elemental sort. Their own faithfulness and love in turn created a wider group in the midst of the hospital's bustle. From them radiated ripples of life that touched all who were joined in the experience.

Groups, I saw again, are where we find our identity. Groups are where our values reside. Groups are where we find inspiration and strength and wisdom. Groups, intimate and honest groups, are the only soil in which the precious flower of faith can grow. And so the parish, if it is to be anything, must be a place of groups.

Decades ago the church in Latin America discovered the special power for nourishing faith that resides in *communidades de base,* small Christian communities. In recent years the North American church has been seeking ways to do the same. Programs such as "Renew," "Cursillo," "Christ Renews his Parish," and a hundred local variations seek to take seriously the truth that faith is transmitted only through face-to-face groups, where people are called by name, where all can speak truthfully and all will listen respectfully. As religious organizations work to create these places of grace, much is learned from the various Twelve-Step Groups, so beautifully manifesting that health is achieved only in sharing and searching together.

Perhaps we have not yet found the forms that suit ideally our particular contexts. But for all that, the objective cannot be lost: to allow the larger structure of parish to be the home for smaller but more powerful groups where discipleship can be truly nurtured.[2]

But this work of creating groups is not easy for many ministers. My own observation, confirmed by others with whom I have shared it, is that people who select ministry as a vocation tend to be persons who enjoy one-on-one interaction, intimacy achieved in giving and receiving love. Consequently, these ministers are, by temperament, most inclined to individual interventions where they provide parishioners with direct service. But the research we have explored in this book suggests that such individual service is relatively less important for the making of disciples. Much more important are those interventions that join people not to the minister but to one another, and that is the sort of activity that most ministers enjoy less.

So an important task for ministers will be assessing the activities with which they choose to fill their day. A standard principle of professional ethics is that professionals should serve first the needs of the client, not the needs of the self. In shaping parochial work, then, ministers will need to ask continually whether their priorities reflect the needs of the people or the preferences of the minister.[3] Do I provide individual counseling because I enjoy this sort of intimate sharing? Or do I invite into existence groups able to provide mutual support in a shared journey of life and faith because I know this strategy to be far more effective? Do I bond people to myself? Or do I join people to one another and then retreat so that their common and communal life may flourish?

These are the kinds of questions that must be faced by any minister who understands that the parish that is effective in helping people to live discipleship is the parish that is a place of groups.

Place of Stories

I once had the opportunity to lead a workshop for all the priests in a rather small diocese. Part of my mandate was to offer reflections on current developments in moral theology. But the planners also hoped that the workshop would serve to support the priests, nourish their bonds with one another, and renew their commitment to shared ministry to the local church. Among the challenges facing the diocese in achieving this goal was the fact that it was a relatively young church, having been separated from a nearby diocese only about twenty years before. Further, the fact that many of the parishes were led by members of religious orders meant that there was a rather large turnover in the population of the local presbyterate. It was difficult even to know one another, let alone to form bonds of collegial service.

As a response to these circumstances, we engaged in a fascinating activity. Along one wall of the meeting room we attached butcher paper, three feet high and perhaps twenty feet long. Down the length of this paper we drew three lines, one above the other. And at intervals along the length we placed vertical lines, six of them, marked with dates: 1940, 1950, 1960, 1970, 1980, 1990. The priests were invited to drag their chairs to this side of the room and to sit comfortably gathered before this large chart. Several of their members were designated scribes, to make notes upon the chart.

The top horizontal line, I explained, represented secular history. The group was invited to recall significant events of the last fifty years. And as they did so, the scribes noted the events along the line, at a point relative to when the event occurred. Many events were obvious: the end of the Second World War or the assassination of John Kennedy. Others had more local significance: the first African American mayor, a particularly demanding winter, the time the river overflowed its banks, and the like. But the exercise brought to mind the world of experiences they all had shared, or that had been shared by significant portions of the group.

Then we moved to the second horizontal line, this time retrieving events in the life of the Roman Catholic Church. Vatican II was recalled. Also the promulgation of *Humanae Vitae*, the election of Pope John Paul II, and so on. Once again, the events were noted at the appropriate spot on the chart. Finally, we moved to the bottom line. And here the group was asked to consider events in the life of the local church. A new energy took life among the priests, as they warmed to this task of remembering. Those who had long been present recalled key events in the life of the diocese. Public events came first, but then more personal moments. "Do you remember the funeral for that old curmudgeon monsignor? We went to the wake to confirm that he was dead! Was that '73 or '74?" "No, it was '75, because it was the year after I was ordained."

What a wonderful sharing! For some priests it was a remembering of the people and of the events that helped give life to this local church. For others, the younger ones and those recently arrived from other locales, it was a chance to understand, to really understand, the spirit of the diocese in which they now served. And in the telling of these tales, in the laughing and remembering and experiencing once again, bonds were deepened, dreams were rekindled, and commitment was reinforced.

Theologian Stanley Hauerwas says that church is a "story-formed community." Because stories rekindle experiences, allowing them to live in our imaginations, a community that seeks to be faithful to its original mission must be forever retelling the stories that gave it life. And so a successful parish must be a place of stories. The stories being shared should include the stories of parish life. There is nothing wrong with recounting the tales of the parish founding, describing in colorful detail the characters who peopled the times that have come and gone. But more deeply, of course, the stories told in the worthy parish are the stories of Jesus.

These stories are told in the pulpit. They are told in the classroom. They are told in prayer groups and support groups and friendship groups. They are told to the elderly to give them hope and to the children to give them vision. They are told by the priests to the people to nourish their faith and by the people to the priests to nourish their hope. And throughout the life of the parish they are told and retold to nourish the love of all.

It is sometimes said that Christian are also "spiritual Semites." We share in the identity of the Jewish people who were called as God's people and remain that people today. Judaism's dream that God will send the gift of a savior is our dream too, and our conviction that this gift now dwells among us does not erase the vision we share with the Jews. For that reason, Christians have much to learn from their Jewish fellows, and to my mind one of the most important lessons is to be found in the ritual of Passover.

First of all, it is fascinating and beautiful that one of the central celebrations of the Jewish calendar is enacted not in the temple or synagogue but in the home, as a family gathers around the table for a common meal. Our embodied faith could hardly be asserted more forcefully. But second, it is profoundly instructive that key components of the ritual are precipitated when the youngest asks the oldest, "Why is this night different from other nights?" Across the generations the question is asked, and across the generations, in the telling of a time-worn but ageless story, the question is answered.

A parish too must be a place of stories. It must be a place where one can ask: What does it all mean? Why are we here? And where are we going? And it must be a place where, in the stories of Jesus, in the stories of disciples gone before, in the stories of the local community, these questions are given answers that are honest and real and life-giving.

Place of Standards

Several years ago I was invited to work with the staff of a local parish, assisting them in setting goals and developing plans for their parochial ministry. In preparing for one of our meetings, I became aware that segments of the parish were involved in a controversy. A newly revised program of preparation for confirmation required the young people, without exception, to attend a series of meetings and participate in a selection of service projects. Some of the parents were upset, noting that the program's schedule of events conflicted with soccer games and other social activities. The staff was divided on the question of what to do.

In the first segment of my meeting with the staff, I guided a process in which they named the values which they considered preeminently important in their parish. The values they named involved qualities such as compassion, openness, unconditional acceptance, and the like. Further discussion confirmed that these values were truly prominent, often mentioned in homilies, prayers of the faithful, articles in the parish bulletin, and the like. At last I interrupted the discussion. "What about the confirmation program?" I asked. "What values does it prioritize?" The values of the program were, of course, quite different: nonnegotiable demand, fidelity, high expectation, commitment, and so on. After further discussion, I summarized a conclusion. "Your parishioners," I suggested, "can be forgiven for their confusion. The fact is that you're giving them a double message. On the one hand, you claim that you stand for unconditional acceptance. On the other hand, you demand perfect performance as the condition for participating in confirmation. Which do you mean? You need to decide, and then to communicate clearly to the people the values you really consider preeminent."

What we have learned about the nature of groups, in the course of this book, confirms that the setting of standards is not at all inappropriate. Indeed, it is an essential project of any group that intends to make a difference. The group that stands for nothing, we learned, truly stands for nothing! Hence, any group that takes itself seriously must define the minimum required for membership and then must enforce the standard they select. The language of utter acceptance, affirmation with no expectation attached, must be revealed as the silliness it is.

Silliness, and often also sabotage. I have observed groups where there actually were no standards. In those cases the group eventually became irrelevant and empty. But I have also observed groups where the verbiage of acceptance disguised a behavior of hidden expectation. There were, in fact, all sorts of rules. Here the result was depression, confusion, and distrust. In neither case was the situation really healthy. Psychologist Evelyn Eaton Whitehead once said that group norms ought to be visible and legible. That is, they should not be hidden where the conscientious person cannot find them. And they should not be ambiguous, so that the willing participant cannot decipher them. Instead, any member equipped with good will and a modicum of intelligence ought to be able to see and understand what it costs to belong to this group.

Of course, setting standards is dangerous. Many commentators fear that the current trend toward a more demanding Catholicism risks turning the church into a sect, imposing an elitism that is a far cry from the gospel message of love. Theologians are removed from teaching positions because of disagreements involving politically sensitive but theologically marginal matters. Rigid standards are imposed in issues of sexual morality with no parallel attempt to enforce the biblical mandates regarding justice, honesty, or compassion. People involved in irregular marriages, for example, are excluded from catechumenate programs; others whose conscientious judgments may have resulted in similarly eccentric ethical positions in business matters or political priorities are not similarly treated. In various ways standards are set that manifest not a clear understanding of the central identity of the Christian community but an arbitrary criterion of personal acceptability.

So the setting of standards is a dangerous business. But to those who care about protecting and cultivating the communal life of discipleship, it cannot be avoided. Thus, like the church as a whole, the individual parish must get clear about what it stands for and where the limits are to be found.

In this regard it may be valuable to recall the fact, reported in chapter 7, that in the early church only three behaviors were judged deserving of excommunication: adultery, homicide, and apostasy. These three behaviors represented direct assaults upon the identity of the community. Since these behaviors constituted a threat to the community itself and since values are transmitted through communities (as we have seen), perpetrators of these acts were excluded from community life. Other behaviors, by contrast, were understood as the stuff of human and faith development within the still-unbroken bond of the discipleship community.

This practice offers a worthy guideline for our time. Inclusion or exclusion of individuals should not depend on the worthiness of the person involved. An individual is not welcomed into the community because of sanctity nor sent forth because of sin. Rather the determining factor is the impact of the behavior upon the community itself. As long as the community survives and maintains its identity as a community of discipleship, all will be well. For that reason and within that criterion, all should be welcome, as well.

Conclusion

Bishop John R. Gorman, a psychologist who has also been an intellectual leader in American Catholicism, once said that human beings need two things: something to believe in and something to belong to. To be successful, the parish must be a place where both these needs are met. The parish must enkindle the faith of its members, leading them to retrieve the vision of Jesus and challenging them to embrace the call of Jesus. Then the parish must provide a place to do just that, inviting its members into a faithful community, a living body of advice and support, a home for commitment and a vehicle for service. Through gifts and groups, through stories and standards, the parish must embrace its own mission and thereby serve the mission to which all of its members are called. As they are called to be disciples, followers of the Lord, so it must be a community of disciples.

If it is this, if the parish is a place where its members find something to believe in and something to belong to, it will truly be what it is meant to be: a place for living discipleship.

Notes

1. This comparison is the creation of John Buscemi, a liturgical theologian and artist. He refers to the church community as an "assembly of strangers," and he points out that this is not necessarily a problem since gatherers at athletic events are the same.

2. Many reflective practitioners are contributing to the exploration of more vibrant visions of parish. I am particularly indebted to the creative work of my former colleague Patrick J. Brennan: for example, *The Evangelizing Parish: Theologies and Strategies for Renewal* (Allen, Tex.: Tabor, 1987); *Re-imagining the Parish: Base Communities, Adulthood, and Family Consciousness* (New York: Crossroad, 1990); *Parishes that Excel: Models of Excellence in Education* (New York: Crossroad, 1992); *Re-imagining Evangelization: Toward the Reign of God and the Communal Parish* (New York: Crossroad, 1995).

3. The insights of professional ethics have not often been applied to the profession of pastoral minister. A noteworthy exception is the fine book by Richard M. Gula, *Ethics in Pastoral Ministry* (New York: Paulist Press, 1996).

4. Stanley Hauerwas, *A Community of Character* (Notre Dame, Ind.: University of Notre Dame Press, 1981), 9.

Conclusion

All authority in heaven and on earth has been given to me. Go therefore and make disciples of all nations, baptizing them . . . and teaching them. . . . And remember, I am with you always, to the end of the age.

—Matt. 28:18-20

Men of Galilee, why do you stand looking up toward heaven? This Jesus, who has been taken up from you into heaven, will come in the same way as you saw him go into heaven.

—Acts 1:11

THE SELECTION FROM THE GOSPEL OF MATTHEW THAT HAS served as our leitmotiv is proclaimed in the liturgy for Ascension Thursday. Not surprisingly, the liturgy pairs this Gospel reading with a first reading from the beginning of the Acts of the Apostles, also quoted above. Both texts highlight two points that will round out our project and bring this book to a close.

Mission

At the beginning, I noted that the primary audience to whom I have addressed this book is the community of ministers, those who have made the making of disciples their life's work. In light of that fact, it is not surprising that our focus has been on what the ministers can do so that the people will *be*. I have not focused as directly on the people's challenge to do.

Yet the departing words of Jesus, as reported by both Matthew and Luke, make clear that all the followers of the Lord are called upon to act. Men—and women—of Galilee are not supposed to stand around staring into the sky, passively waiting for God to continue the direct "interventionist" acts of salvation that characterized the life of Jesus. Quite the contrary, they are all expected to participate in the Lord's work, baptizing and teaching the world.

To say this is to spotlight the missionary aspect of the church. Scholars sometimes describe the life of the church as involving three activities: *leitourgia, koinōnia, diakonia* (worship, community, service). But they also sometimes remind us that the three are not altogether equal. Actually, we could describe the life of discipleship as involving worship and service, love of God and neighbor. Then we could note that, given the social nature of the human person, both of these projects demand a communal home. In any case, service is central. Ministry and community are ultimately to express themselves in mission. Indeed, it is worth noting that in gathering followers to himself, Jesus was not unlike many of the ancient rabbis. It was when he sent those followers away from himself, authorizing them to act in his name, that he broke ranks with the customary arrangement.

And this call to mission is not pious emptiness. It has a three-faceted sharp edge to it: poetry, prophecy, and practicality.

For one thing, mission means that for followers of Jesus a poet's passion for the world is an essential component of faith. I think it was Teilhard de Chardin who said: "because I am a Christian, nothing human is foreign to me." An appreciation for all of creation, for nature and science, for art and technology—a lust for life belongs to the essence of Christianity. After all, the disciple is a follower of Jesus, but Jesus is the Son of the one who made all things. The God of redemption and the God of creation are the same god, and they must not be pitted against each other. So a poet's view of life is obligatory.

But also a prophet's view. The brokenness of the world is obvious for all to see. This is what Catholic theology acknowledges in the doctrine of original sin. To be sure, that personal culpability that we call actual sin is part of every life. But more radical yet is that captivity in which all of creation and all of God's creatures are trapped. Good people hurt one another. Structures, which ought either to help or, at the least, to be neutral, actually harm and enslave and destroy. Injury that would never be inflicted with intentionality is regularly inflicted because of oversight and ignorance, fatigue and indifference.

So the prophet's challenge, the prophet's objection, the prophet's countercultural alternative is also part of the disciple's mission. Recent church documents call for a "preferential option for the poor." Some commentators have found this offensive, claiming that one who sees all people as God's children ought to exhibit an even-handedness, preferring no one in particular. But the church's teaching is more realistic. It knows that, in the world as it exists, there is no such thing as a level playing field. Indeed, in things as they are, there is a preferential option for the rich. Even to attempt true even-handedness, then, one must begin with a bias toward the downtrodden. This is the prophet's message.

Mission also, in the third place, requires a practitioner's view. For a long time and in many settings, there has been a resistance to the use of human knowledge in service to religious work. Let me give several examples.

Father Andrew Greeley has often commented on the tendency to dispose of sociological research as if God's action in the world would not be assisted by accurate understanding. And there is no denying that many studies of church life undertaken by him, and by others, have been allowed to exercise paltry influence in developing ministry for our time. Similarly, in a Vatican discussion of the ethics of artificial contraception some years ago, I noted that statistics on the widespread lack of understanding of the teaching were rejected with the comment: "We don't write doctrine through surveys." Of course we don't. But when the people being surveyed are the People of God who are struggling to live lives of discipleship with sincerity and commitment, then their inability to understand and appreciate a teaching often reasserted is theologically (and not just sociologically) significant. And research that exposes the lack of understanding is itself a medium through which God's truth is being revealed.

As another example, I was once invited to speak to an audience of ministers on the topic "Professional and Pastoral." The presumption was that these two are often seen as being in conflict, and the comments of the audience confirmed that presumption. My argument was that they are complements, that genuine professionalism, as "secular" as that sounds, would serve well the pastoral task. Indeed, with sadness I noted many examples where "mere professionals" enacted principles of respect, fairness, competence, and commitment that put many pastoral persons to shame. So attempts to polarize the human and the spiritual, and to defend the polarization on theological grounds, are caricatures indeed.

The point is that one who accepts Jesus' call to mission to the world uses every tool available. That is the understanding that has prompted this book. We have delved into the insights of the social sciences because I believe with a religious faith that the God of salvation is also the God of creation and that the work of discipleship will only be done well where every available source of insight is exploited.

So there is an activism to discipleship, an activism of poetry and prophecy and practicality. There is a mission at its core. It is about this that ministers teach; it is for this work that ministers baptize; it is to the task of proclaiming this that ministers are sent when they are told to go and "make disciples."

Letting Go

But for all that, the full burden of this work does not rest on our shoulders. Throughout Christian history, two heresies have continually recurred. Though particular examples have their own names, in general the heresies can be understood as Quietism and Pelagianism. Quietism presumes that since God is ultimately in charge, I can do nothing and consequently should do nothing. Pelagianism, on the other hand, presumes that since God has given us freedom, the achievement of salvation truly and fully resides in my hands such that I am truly "on my own."

In these comments I want to resist the heresy of Pelagianism. No matter how we understand the mission to which all of Jesus' followers are called, we cannot understand it as meaning that the project is fully our own. In the end, the healing and salvation of God's world reside in God's hands. The act of loving service rides on the wings of God's grace. The disciple can "go and baptize" only because the disciple has been "sent."

Luke has the angels tell Jesus' followers not to stand around. But they also assure them that Jesus "will come in the same way as you saw him go." And Matthew puts in Jesus' mouth not only the words of mission but also the words of promise: "know that I will be with you."

If this is a true and important insight for all those willing to be disciples of the Lord, it is just as true and important for all those who set out to make disciples of the Lord. In this book's introduction, I acknowledged the presumptuousness of our title. "Making Disciples" sounds as Pelagian as anything I've ever heard! I defended the title by pointing out that it was Jesus, as reported by Matthew, who told us to do just that.

At the end, however, I want to revisit that presumptuous title, noting also that the Jesus who told us to do it, also told us that we would not do it alone. This is important. If ministers sometimes fail in their task by abandoning their important work, I think they more often fail by allowing themselves to imagine that the work is entirely theirs. And because they imagine this, they cannot imagine letting go. So often I have observed dedicated ministers, ordained and otherwise, suffering in tremendously inhospitable settings. They do all sorts of things to survive the setting; when this fails, they resort to complaining about the setting. But they seem to find it almost impossible to let go of the setting.

Imagine, if you will, that this minister is holding a hand above a burning candle. The arrangement causes pain. So the minister prays: "Dear God, save me from this pain." I believe the prayer is answered; the Spirit of God does respond. I suppose that sometimes the Spirit responds by entering the room as a burst of wind, as at Pentecost, which extinguishes the candle and so removes the pain. But more often, I suspect, the Spirit responds by entering the room as a gentle whisper of wind, moving to the minister's ear and declaring softly, "Move your hand, dummy!"

This incredible resistance to moving is, I believe, a manifestation of Pelagianism, a refusal to admit that the work is finally God's and not ours. Against this we must hear the balanced words of Matthew and Luke, calling for commitment but also asserting the primacy of God's action.

In the pages of this book I have had occasion to reflect on events surrounding the death of Cardinal Joseph Bernardin. It appears that many people were inspired by his willingness to refer to death as "my friend," by the courage and patience with which he accepted the approaching end of his life. But I believe that for many ministers the inspiration came from something slightly different. Cardinal Bernardin was known as a "churchman." His actions revealed that he felt a profound responsibility for the life of the church, struggling to maintain unity, working to achieve compromise, endeavoring to appreciate the needs and contributions of all. If anything, then, the general pattern of Cardinal Bernardin's life might suggest that his characteristic temptation would be Pelagianism, so much did he take on responsibility for the church.

For that very reason, then, there was a profound inspiration to be found in the Cardinal's ability to "let go." He seemed able to accept that envisioned works would not take place, to release the many activities of the diocese from his control, and, in many different ways, to put the fate of the church back in God's hands. So must every minister.

Conclusion

The message of this book, then, invites both to skillful action and spiritual acceptance, to taking personal responsibility and to knowing that God is always with us. It is a message of theology and social science, of insight and experience. It is a message of mission and of letting go.

And it is a message of hope. I really do want to influence the students that I teach. I regret that I failed to do that in the early years of my teaching. And I intend to make every effort to succeed in doing that in the future. I plan to use all the skill that I have, all the insight that I can collect, all the wisdom that resides in the worlds of scholarship, for the task of making disciples. And I plan to teach well the ministerial students whom I serve, so that they in turn can make disciples wherever they go.

But I know that I will succeed only in part. And, though I would often prefer to ignore the fact, I know that, even when I succeed, the success will finally be not the product of perseverance but the gift of grace. And I know that, while God expects all this careful thinking and skillful work, God will use these things in God's own ways, which I will never fully understand.

So the message is a message of hope. It begins in the call to "make disciples." But it rests finally in the announcement that "this Jesus, who has been taken up from you into heaven, will come in the same way."

Index